# The Way of the Spirits
# Shinto: From the Self to the Sacred

Haruki Nishimura

BOOKLAS
PUBLISHING

**Original Title:**
*The Way of the Spirits: Shinto – From the Self to the Sacred*
**Copyright © 2024, published by Luiz Antonio dos Santos ME.**
This book is a non-fiction work exploring the spiritual principles and practices of Shinto. Through a comprehensive and poetic approach, the author offers insight into Japanese ancestral wisdom, highlighting themes such as purity, harmony, and the sacredness of nature.
**1st Edition**
**Production Team**
Author: Haruki Nishimura
Editor: Luiz Santos
Cover Design: Studios Booklas / Amari Keene
Consultant: Dorian Lest
Researchers: Hana Kurosu / Felix Nomura / Mireille Kaen
Layout Design: Solen Ravis

**Publication and Identification**
*The Way of the Spirits: Shinto – From the Self to the Sacred*
Booklas, 2024
Categories: Spirituality / Japanese Culture
DDC: 299.56 – CDU: 299.561
All rights reserved to:
Luiz Antonio dos Santos ME / Booklas
No part of this book may be reproduced, stored in a retrieval system, or transmitted in any form or by any means—electronic, mechanical, photocopying, recording, or otherwise—without the prior written permission of the copyright holder.

# Summary

Index Sistematic ........................................................................... 5
Prologue ....................................................................................... 9
Chapter 1   The Way of the Kami ........................................... 13
Chapter 2   Ancestral Origin .................................................... 19
Chapter 3   Sacred Nature ........................................................ 25
Chapter 4   Rites of Purity ....................................................... 31
Chapter 5   Sacred Spaces ........................................................ 37
Chapter 6   Offerings and Prayers .......................................... 43
Chapter 7   Seasonal Festivals ................................................. 49
Chapter 8   Protector Gods ...................................................... 55
Chapter 9   The Home Altar .................................................... 61
Chapter 10  Everyday Religion ................................................ 67
Chapter 11  Roles of the Priest ................................................ 72
Chapter 12  Female Priesthood ................................................ 78
Chapter 13  Sacred Dances ....................................................... 84
Chapter 14  Sounds and Symbols ............................................ 90
Chapter 15  Rites of Passage .................................................... 95
Chapter 16  The Way of the Family ..................................... 100
Chapter 17  Community Harmony ........................................ 105
Chapter 18  Virtues of the Heart ........................................... 110
Chapter 19  Education and Character ................................... 115
Chapter 20  Work as Offering ................................................ 120
Chapter 21  The Way of Prosperity ...................................... 125
Chapter 22  Circle of the Seasons ......................................... 131

Chapter 23  Shrines Abroad ..................................................... 135
Chapter 24  Silent Conversion ................................................. 140
Chapter 25  Ancestral Wisdom ................................................ 145
Chapter 26  Inner Path .............................................................. 150
Chapter 27  Beauty as Path ...................................................... 155
Chapter 28  Spirit of Gratitude ................................................. 160
Chapter 29  The Way of Harmony ........................................... 165
Chapter 30  Eternity of the Kami ............................................. 170
Chapter 31  Wisdom of the Cycles .......................................... 174
Chapter 32  The Living Legacy ............................................... 179
Epilogue .................................................................................. 183

# Index Sistematic

Chapter 1: The Way of the Kami - Introduces Shinto as the Way of the Kami, explaining the nature of these deities and the principles of harmony and purity.

Chapter 2: Ancestral Origin - Details the Shinto creation myths, the origin of primordial kami, and the birth of central deities like Amaterasu.

Chapter 3: Sacred Nature - Explores the Shinto view of nature as a sacred space intrinsically inhabited by kami.

Chapter 4: Rites of Purity - Discusses the importance of purity (kiyome) and purification rites (misogi, harae) for removing impurity (kegare) and connecting with the kami.

Chapter 5: Sacred Spaces - Describes Shinto shrines (jinja), their structure (like the torii), atmosphere, and function as community spiritual centers.

Chapter 6: Offerings and Prayers - Explains the practices of offerings (shinsen) and prayers (norito), emphasizing sincerity (magokoro) as the essential element.

Chapter 7: Seasonal Festivals - Details seasonal festivals (matsuri), like Shōgatsu and Setsubun, and their connection to natural cycles and community renewal.

Chapter 8: Protector Gods - Introduces different types of kami, especially ujigami (local protectors) and specific deities like Inari and Hachiman.

Chapter 9: The Home Altar - Focuses on the kamidana, the domestic Shinto altar, describing its setup, daily offerings, and role in home spirituality.

Chapter 10: Everyday Religion - Illustrates how Shinto spirituality manifests in daily life through simple gestures, attitudes, and customs.

Chapter 11: Roles of the Priest - Describes the functions of the Shinto priest (kannushi), emphasizing their role as guardians of purity and rituals.

Chapter 12: Female Priesthood - Discusses the historical and current role of women in Shinto, like the miko (ritual assistants) and ordained priestesses.

Chapter 13: Sacred Dances - Explores kagura, the sacred Shinto dance, its mythical origin, and its function as a ritual invocation of the kami.

Chapter 14: Sounds and Symbols - Examines the importance of sounds (bells, clapping, drums) and visual symbols (torii, shimenawa) in Shinto practice and communication.

Chapter 15: Rites of Passage - Details Shinto ceremonies marking life stages, such as birth (hatsumiyamairi), childhood (Shichi-Go-San), and marriage.

Chapter 16: The Way of the Family - Discusses the family as a sacred unit, emphasizing ancestor veneration and harmony (wa) in the home.

Chapter 17: Community Harmony - Focuses on wa (harmony) within the community, centered on the local shrine and the ujigami (protector kami).

Chapter 18: Virtues of the Heart - Explores the core ethical values of Shinto, like makoto (sincerity), purity, respect, and righteousness.

Chapter 19: Education and Character - Describes how Shinto principles influence Japanese education, focusing on character formation through example and discipline.

Chapter 20: Work as Offering - Presents the Shinto view of work as a spiritual practice and offering (kodawari), valuing dedication and quality.

Chapter 21: The Way of Prosperity - Explains prosperity in Shinto as multifaceted flourishing resulting from harmony with the kami and nature.

Chapter 22: Circle of the Seasons - Discusses the Shinto perception of time as cyclical, emphasizing alignment with the rhythm of the seasons.

Chapter 23: Shrines Abroad - Covers the presence and adaptation of Shinto shrines and practices outside Japan, highlighting the universality of the kami.

Chapter 24: Silent Conversion - Explains that adherence to Shinto is an internal process of attunement and practice, not requiring formal conversion.

Chapter 25: Ancestral Wisdom - Focuses on Shinto myths as living sources of spiritual wisdom about the kami, nature, and the soul.

Chapter 26: Inner Path - Describes the contemplative dimension of Shinto, cultivated through presence and listening to nature.

Chapter 27: Beauty as Path - Explores the role of beauty, particularly the wabi-sabi aesthetic, as a spiritual path in Shinto.

Chapter 28: Spirit of Gratitude - Highlights gratitude as a central force and continuous state of consciousness in Shinto.

Chapter 29: The Way of Harmony - Centers on wa (harmony) as a fundamental principle, encompassing balance with nature, others, and the kami.

Chapter 30: Eternity of the Kami - Discusses the Shinto concept of eternity as continuity within cycles, including the permanence of kami and ancestors.

Chapter 31: Wisdom of the Cycles - Deepens the understanding of cyclical time, emphasizing acceptance of life's phases and renewal.

Chapter 32: The Living Legacy - Concludes by reaffirming Shinto as a living spiritual path, its legacy residing in everyday reverence and harmony.

# Prologue

There are places in the world where the unseen is not absence—it is presence. Where every stone, every leaf, and every breath of wind carries a spark of the sacred. Japan is one such place.

In an island archipelago that lives between earthquakes and silences, between strict discipline and gentle contemplation, stands a civilization that endures time not with force, but with reverence. A nation that found prosperity not only in skyscrapers or technological advances but, above all, in the delicacy of a gesture, the depth of a rite, the harmony with what pulses unseen.

Why do the Japanese live longer? Smile more? Fall ill less often? Their gardens speak in silence; their shrines whisper to the attentive. Why?

Is this merely the reflection of a functional culture, a rigorous ethic, a refined aesthetic? Or is there something deeper sustaining such harmony?

The answer—like all that is sacred—does not lie on the surface.

This book unveils an ancestral secret. A secret guarded not by fear, but protected by subtlety. Because it is not a belief system or a set of rules. It is a way of seeing the world. Of feeling the world. Of *being* in the world.

Discover what lies behind Japanese longevity. Awaken to the spirituality that permeates the daily lives of millions who, even without declaring themselves religious, live in deep harmony with forces that transcend logical understanding.

This ancient wisdom presented here does not shout. It whispers. It does not impose. It invites.

Like the dew forming on leaves before dawn, it demands presence to be perceived. And when perceived, it transforms. It transforms the gaze, the gesture, the body, the home, the life.

Each chapter of this book is a portal. A symbolic *torii* you pass through to access not another world, but another way of inhabiting *this* one.

Here, you will be introduced to Shinto not as an exotic religion, but as a universal spiritual language—a call to reconnect with nature, with ancestors, with silence, and above all, with your *magokoro*: the true heart.

Do not expect doctrines. What you will find are revelations. Surprising revelations about how spirit can inhabit matter, how time can be circular, how work can be an offering, and how beauty can be a path.

Shinto, as presented here, offers no promises. It offers practices. Simple, yet sacred practices.

The way of washing hands, crossing a gate, looking at a flower, cleaning the home, being silent—everything can be ritual, everything can be communion. Everything can be a path.

There is a call to sensitivity in this work. An invitation for you to become not just a reader, but a devotee of the present moment. So that you finally recognize that it is not necessary to be in Japan to live like a spiritual Japanese person. It is enough to look around with reverence. Enough to breathe with awareness. Enough to recognize that the falling leaf, the rising sun, the flowing tear—all are manifestations of a divine that inhabits the everyday.

This book is an offering. And by reading it, you are not just receiving content—you are attuning yourself to a vibrational field that has sustained one of the most harmonious cultures on the planet for centuries.

You will be guided through founding myths, sacred dances, purification rituals, collective celebrations that not only entertain but teach how to live with soul.

Make no mistake: what is shared here is not an ethnographic curiosity. It is wisdom that touches the human soul at any latitude.

In times of crisis, speed, and dispersion, this book presents itself as a refuge. But more than that: as a fresh start.

Allow yourself to pass through the invisible portals of the sacred. Allow yourself to see with new eyes. Allow yourself to be touched by a spirituality that does not separate heaven from earth, nor spirit from body. Here, all is one. All is *kami*. All is an opportunity for reconnection.

By the end of the reading, you will not be the same. And the world, which was already sacred, will finally be recognized as such by you.
Luiz Santos Editor

# Chapter 1
# The Way of the Kami

The world is not just a stage of matter and motion, but a vast realm where the unseen whispers through leaves, rivers, and breezes. Ancestral Japan, nestled between volcanic mountains and deep seas, recognized this whisper millennia ago. From it emerged one of humanity's most unique and ethereal spiritual visions: Shinto.

Unlike major Western religions or Eastern philosophical systems, Shinto is not built on imposing dogmas or doctrines. It does not impose a single truth, nor does it present a savior to be followed. Instead, it offers a path of perception—a sensitive spiritual trail where the sacred reveals itself in daily life, in natural cycles, and in the intimate relationship between human beings and the cosmos. It is the Way of the Kami.

"Kami" is a word that defies precise translation. Some interpret it as "gods," others as "spirits," but neither expression captures its true depth. Kami are presences, potencies, consciousnesses manifesting *in* things and *beyond* them. A mountain can be a kami; an ancient tree, a river winding silently among stones, the raw force of a typhoon, the ephemeral brilliance of a falling cherry blossom—all can contain or *be* a kami.

But not just visible nature: revered ancestors, heroes of the past, clan founders—all can ascend to this spiritual state. The world, seen through Shinto eyes, is profoundly animated—and there is no radical separation between the spiritual and the material.

Calling Shinto a "religion" sometimes narrows its scope. It is more accurate to understand it as a way of being in the world, a form of relationship between the self and the unseen, between humans and the environment. There are no scriptures revealed by unique, all-powerful gods, nor a central figure demanding exclusive worship. There are also no promises of eternal salvation or infernal punishments. Instead, there is an invitation to harmony—*wa*—and purity—*kiyome*. Life is lived in its fullness, and the sacred is a continuity of the everyday, not its denial or transcendence.

The Way of the Kami begins with attention. Observing a stone, not as an object, but as a presence. Feeling the wind and perceiving its soul. Hearing the rain, not as incidental sound, but as a murmur that touches the spirit. This perception, developed over time and with care, opens the soul to the world of the kami. They do not shout. They do not impose. They are like echoes responding to sincere reverence. The world, in this sense, becomes not just a place to live, but a sanctuary in itself.

This path does not demand blind faith. It demands sensitivity. It demands inner integrity, known as *magokoro*—the "true heart," expressed in simple, sincere actions. Reverence for a kami can be shown with a respectfully offered branch of *sakaki*, a silent prayer under a waterfall, or even careful posture while cleaning the entrance of one's home. Everything is expression. Everything is offering. And therefore, everything can be sacred.

Shinto flourished in an archipelago where natural forces are immense and untamable. Earthquakes, typhoons, tsunamis, and eruptions shaped not only the geography but the spirit of the people. Faced with this grand and unpredictable nature, humans do not impose themselves. They observe, revere, and learn to flow. The spirituality of the Japanese, shaped by Shinto, recognizes this dependence on the environment and develops a relationship of profound gratitude and respect with it. Hence the ecological sense emanating from traditional culture: it is not fashion, it is worldview. When one understands that a river has spirit, polluting it becomes sacrilege. When one understands that a mountain is the abode of gods, its devastation is a profanation. Shinto did not need to create ecological treaties, because its vision was already inherently ecological. Nature is not 'resources'—it is kinship. Every being, every plant, every phenomenon is part of a great cosmic family, where humans do not occupy a throne, but a place of coexistence.

This sensitivity, so deeply ingrained in Japanese culture, transcends time. Even today, amidst skyscrapers, neon lights, and high-speed trains, the Way of the Kami remains. A small shrine might be seen on a busy Tokyo corner. A solitary *torii* stands between buildings, marking the passage to a tiny shrine, yet brimming with presence. Young people still make silent offerings; elders still revere sacred trees with clasped hands. The modern and the archaic intertwine, not in opposition, but in continuity.

In Shinto, there is no conversion. No one becomes Shinto by signing a paper or reciting a formula. One becomes Shinto by living with reverence. By giving thanks for a meal, purifying oneself before entering a shrine, greeting the new day with respect. It is a silent, intimate, daily practice. Many Japanese do not even declare themselves religious, yet they live Shinto in every gesture. This confuses Western scholars accustomed to systems where religious identity is a clear label. In Japan, it is as fluid as the mist over rice paddies at dawn.

The Way of the Kami is also a path of purity. But not in the moralistic sense the West often attributes to the word. Purity in Shinto refers to energetic cleansing, lightness of being, clearing the soul so the kami can approach. Impurity, or *kegare*, is anything that disturbs this harmony—deep sadness, death, illness, emotional chaos. Therefore, there are many rites of purification: baths, offerings, prayers, and silences. The body, the environment, and the spirit must be in consonance for the sacred to manifest fully.

The world is full of kami, say the ancients. And indeed it is. But it requires eyes that see, ears that hear, and a heart that understands. Shinto, unlike many religions, does not wish to convert. It invites. Its voice does not shout; it whispers. And what it says is simple, yet transformative: everything is sacred. Every leaf, every tear, every gesture can be a link to the divine, if there is sincerity and attention. Shinto is an art of living—and living well, with gratitude, respect, and wonder.

The Western reader approaching this path may seek answers. But they will find, first, a mirror. And in it, they will see not the face of a god demanding worship, but the reflection of a world awaiting reverence. The tree growing in the backyard, the river flowing near home, the sky at dawn—all are imbued with the presence the Japanese called kami. And the heart, recognizing this presence, also transforms.

Shinto, therefore, calls us to a state of radical attention, where living is essentially a poetic act. It is not about seeking a transcendent logic or a totalizing explanation of the universe, but about cultivating a constant listening to what vibrates silently in reality. This listening is not just metaphysical, but ethical: it implies responsibility, humility, and reciprocity with all that lives and pulses. In this sense, the Way of the Kami is not only a spiritual path but also a training of sensitivity—a continuous learning of how to inhabit the world with delicacy and reverence. Unlike traditions that see the sacred as distant or reserved for grand temples, here the sacred insinuates itself into the ordinary, asking only for an awakened gaze.

This way of being in the world does not deny suffering but embraces it as part of the flow. Losses, absences, and impurities are not curses to be avoided, but states to be recognized, purified, and traversed with courage and serenity. Shinto does not teach to eliminate chaos, but to restore harmony whenever it is broken. Life is seen as a dynamic field of forces, where the human role is one of constant harmonization. In this process, ritual is not empty formalism but a vital practice, where body, gesture, and intention weave bridges between the visible and the invisible. Thus, even the simplest acts—like washing hands before a prayer—gain spiritual and poetic density.

Ultimately, the Way of the Kami points not to a final destination, but to a continuous journey of attunement with the world. A journey without demands of faith, but rich in demands of presence. Being whole in each moment, with *magokoro* pulsating in every gesture, is the deepest offering one can make. And when this true heart meets the world, the world responds. Not with thunderous miracles, but with the subtle grace of a caressing breeze, light filtering through leaves, peace blooming for no apparent reason. And then we understand: living with the kami is, above all, an art of loving the world in its entirety.

# Chapter 2
# Ancestral Origin

Before there were kings, temples, or names, there was the void. Not the void of absence, but a void full of potency, where the unseen fermented in silence. From this ancestral principle, indistinct and mysterious, emerged the first kami. They were not born as humans, nor did they assume definite forms. They were presences, cosmic vibrations, inhabiting the plane of the unseen, giving rise to what is now known as the world.

The origins of Shinto are intertwined with Japanese mythology recorded in the classic texts *Kojiki* ('Records of Ancient Matters,' compiled in 712) and *Nihon Shoki* ('Chronicles of Japan,' completed in 720). These works are not just repositories of ancient myths—they are living expressions of a worldview where the spiritual and physical are inseparable. Their accounts do not claim to be 'factual history,' as understood by modern thought, but reveal a deeper truth: the sacred connection between the land, the people, and the gods.

In the beginning, when heaven and earth were not yet separated, the first celestial kami emerged. They existed on the highest plane of reality, in an abode known as *Takamagahara*, the High Celestial Plain. Among these first beings, three primordial kami stand out: Ame-no-Minakanushi, Takamimusubi, and Kamimusubi. They did not act, did not speak, merely existed—silent and sublime, like archetypes of creation.

Over time, other kami emerged, and among them, finally, the creator gods of the earth: Izanagi-no-Mikoto and Izanami-no-Mikoto. Their figures are central to Shinto cosmogony. Tasked with forming the physical world, they received from the celestial deities a sacred, jewel-encrusted spear—the *Ame-no-Nuboko*. Positioned on the bridge between the heavens and the primordial chaos, *Ame-no-Ukihashi*, they dipped the spear into the indistinct sea below. As they lifted it, viscous drops fell from its tip and solidified, forming the first land: the island of Onogoro-shima.

It was there that Izanagi and Izanami descended, and there they united to begin the creation of the other islands of Japan, in a ritual blending sacred eroticism and divine fertility. The dance around the central pillar, the meeting of gazes and words, the exchange of masculine and feminine energies—all symbolize the union of opposing and complementary forces. From this union were born the islands of the Japanese archipelago and a vast lineage of kami, each related to natural and social aspects: seas, rivers, mountains, winds, trees, fire.

However, not everything flowed without tragedy. Giving birth to the fire kami, Kagutsuchi, Izanami suffered fatal burns. Her body was consumed by pain and death, and she descended to the dark realm of *Yomi*, the world of the dead. Izanagi, overcome with despair, tried to rescue her, but upon finding her decomposed, he broke the pact of silence and was driven from that world by his beloved, transformed into wrath.

Izanagi's escape from Yomi marks a rupture: the presence of death in the world, the impurity that contaminates the living, and the need for purification. Upon returning to the world of the living, Izanagi performs a purification ritual—the first *misogi*—immersing himself in a river to rid himself of the impurities contracted in the underworld. And it is at this moment that the three most important gods of the Shinto pantheon are born: Amaterasu-ōmikami (goddess of the sun), from his left eye; Tsukuyomi (god of the moon), from his right eye; and Susanoo (god of storms and the sea), from his nose.

These three celestial gods inherited different aspects of the cosmos and starred in the dramas that would shape the relationship between the divine and the human. Amaterasu, the most revered of all, shines not only as the physical sun but as spiritual light. She becomes the ancestor of the Japanese imperial family and the source of the throne's divine legitimacy. Her abode in *Takamagahara* is a symbol of order, harmony, and clarity.

Her most famous myth, however, is that of her retreat into the cave. After a conflict with her brother Susanoo—marked by destruction, aggression, and disrespect—Amaterasu hides in a cave, plunging the world into darkness. Chaos ensues, and all the kami gather to bring her back. With ritual dances, laughter, and offerings, they manage to attract her attention until she peeks out curiously. At that moment, a mirror is held up, and upon seeing her reflection, she is enchanted and emerges. Light returns to the world.

This myth is more than a tale. It speaks of the importance of beauty, celebration, and collectivity as ways to restore order. It shows that light can be lost when imbalance reigns, and that restoration requires art, intelligence, and communion.

Amaterasu's relationship with humans is direct. According to tradition, she sent her grandson, Ninigi-no-Mikoto, to govern the earth. To him, she entrusted three sacred treasures: the mirror (symbolizing wisdom and introspection), the sword (courage and just action), and the curved jewel (benevolence and connection). These objects, known as the Three Imperial Treasures, are still symbols of the Japanese throne today. Ninigi's great-grandson, Jimmu Tenno, would become the first emperor of Japan, establishing the imperial lineage directly descended from the sun goddess.

This connection between divinity and humanity is crucial. It dissolves the rigid separation between the sacred and the profane. In Shinto, humans can, through virtuous actions and an upright life, become kami. Revered ancestors, heroes who marked their communities' history, clan founders—all can be elevated to spiritual status. Death is not the end, but a transition. Ancestry is alive, present, active. The worship of ancestors is not nostalgia, but the continuity of spiritual presence in the world.

Understanding the mythical origin of Japan and the gods is not, therefore, an intellectual or literary exercise. It is a way of living in consonance with the truth of the cosmos, recognizing the sacredness of the land, family ties, and the natural order. Every rite, every ceremonial gesture, echoes the steps of Izanagi, the teachings of Amaterasu, the ardor of Susanoo. Shinto tradition does not distance itself from mythology—it updates it with every offering, every festival, every reverence made with a sincere heart.

Looking at this cosmogony, we realize that Shinto seeks not a separation between the human and the divine, but rather a continuous network of relationships, where everything that exists is a manifestation and extension of the primordial energy of the kami. There is no rigid hierarchy between heaven and earth, but a constant flow between worlds, woven by symbolic narratives that guide the way of being, acting, and belonging.

Ancestral memory thus becomes a field of revelations that still pulses, teaching that the past is not closed—it breathes through the mountains, rivers, and practices transmitted from generation to generation. And it is in this intertwining that Japan, more than a nation, reveals itself as a sacred landscape, shaped by divine hands and human hearts in communion.

The birth of the gods and islands, the mythical dramas between celestial siblings, and the bestowal of the imperial treasures compose a tapestry that anchors the present in eternity. Instead of dogmas, Shinto offers living myths capable of dialoguing with everyday life, nurturing the soul and the sense of belonging. Each mythical account brings not only the genesis of a people but a subtle pedagogy about balance, courage, reverence, and purification. Through these stories, one understands that creation is not a single, finished act, but a continuous process, remade in rituals, ethics, and the aesthetics of living. The world, from this perspective, is not raw data to be dominated, but a gift to be honored.

Thus, returning to the origin is more than revisiting a mythical time—it is reactivating the listening for what has always been present: the sacredness permeating the world. Shinto teaches that we are children of heaven and earth, heirs to the light of Amaterasu and the cry of Izanagi. By recognizing this heritage, humans reintegrate into the cosmic order not as dominators, but as caretakers and celebrants. The ancestral origin, far from being a distant point, is a presence that sustains the now. And it is in this recognition that the spiritual path strengthens, allowing every gesture, however simple, to become an echo of primordial creation.

# Chapter 3
# Sacred Nature

The breeze passing through an ancient forest, the silence of a lake at dusk, the distant sound of cicadas on a Japanese summer day—all this is not merely natural phenomenon. For those walking the Way of the Kami, they are direct manifestations of the sacred. Nature, in all its variety and rhythm, is not just an object of aesthetic or scientific contemplation. It is, above all, spiritual territory. In Shinto, nature does not symbolize the divine—it *contains* it. This perception is not philosophical or theoretical, but deeply visceral. To live according to Shinto is to live immersed in a world where every stone and every leaf carries spirit.

The concept permeating this view is called *shinrabanshō*—a word that comprehensively designates the totality of things in the universe. At its core is the idea that everything that exists possesses spirit, life force, consciousness. Nothing is truly inert. A river flowing through valleys is not just moving water: it possesses soul, memory, will. A mountain is not mere geological formation: it is a sacred entity, abode of ancient kami. A gnarled pine resisting snow is not just a resilient plant, but a silent master of balance and beauty.

This profoundly ecological spirituality is not doctrinated. It is lived. From childhood, the traditional Japanese learns to view with respect what grows, runs, flies, moves, or transforms in the landscape. Daily gestures reflect this reverence: the way a garden is cleaned, how a *torii* is crossed with correct posture, how the sound of rain is listened to in silence. Everything carries intention. And this intention connects the human being to the unseen world of the kami.

Among the countless places considered sacred, some stand out as true centers of spiritual power. Mountains like Fujisan, the revered Mount Fuji, are not just geographical landmarks but points of intersection between worlds. Its altitude, symmetrical shape, imposing presence—all invite reverence. Many pilgrims climbing Mount Fuji do so not for sport or physical challenge, but as a ritual of connection. The ascent is an inner climb, a reunion with the heart of earth and sky. Rivers like the Kamo in Kyoto carry centuries of offerings, silent prayers, ritual baths. Ancient trees, like the great cedars found in shrines such as Toshogu or Kumano, are wrapped with rice straw ropes, called *shimenawa*—a visible sign that a kami dwells there. Such trees are not touched without permission. Their roots are respected, their space kept clean, and their presence welcomed with solemnity.

Animals also participate in this web of meanings. The fox (*kitsune*) is the messenger of Inari, kami of fertility and harvest. Deer, like those roaming freely in the Nara sanctuary, are considered emissaries of the gods. Cranes, carp, serpents—all possess spiritual meanings transcending their appearance. Respect for animals is not just moral—it is ritual. They are part of the world's spiritual community.

But not only the grand elements of nature are revered. Shinto teaches to see the extraordinary in the ordinary. A bamboo grove dancing in the wind, moss growing silently among stones, a flower blooming for just a few days—everything has value, everything expresses a lesson. This aesthetic and spiritual sensitivity is revealed in the tradition of *hanami*, the contemplation of cherry blossoms. When the *sakura* bloom, there is a collective call to contemplate ephemeral beauty. Families gather under the trees, celebrate, sing, toast, but always with a note of reverence. The flower that lasts so briefly teaches about impermanence, the value of now, beauty that does not cling. This connection with nature even shapes language. Terms like *mono no aware*—the sweet melancholy born from awareness of transience—reveal a soul moved by that which does not last. The natural world, being unstable and perishable, is also precious. And for that very reason, profoundly sacred.

In many shrines, there are no statues. Instead, there is a stone, a mirror, or just empty space surrounded by trees. This is not absence. It is refined presence. The kami needs no form to exist. It manifests in the sound of the bell, the scent of incense, the gleam of running water. The absence of image is a way of saying: look deeper. See beyond the surface. Feel.

Contemplation of nature in Shinto is more than a healthy habit. It is a form of prayer. There is no need for words, for supplications. The simple act of being before the sea, listening to birds at dawn, touching the rough bark of an ancient tree—all express religiosity. And this spirituality is accessible. It requires no monumental temples, no priestly training. Just an attentive heart. Just presence.

This vision also shaped architecture, gardens, arts. A traditional Japanese garden seeks not to dominate nature, but to dialogue with it. Stones are placed precisely not to show off, but to reveal the spirit of the place. Artificial lakes are made with such harmony they seem natural. Each tree is pruned to flourish in its most authentic form. Nothing is artificial—everything seeks the truth of nature.

Modern ecology, in its quest to restore connection with the earth, finds an ancestral model in Shinto. Respect for water, earth, air, fire—elements not as resources, but as partners—resonates strongly in a time of environmental crisis. Shinto never needed to proclaim an ecological discourse because its essence was already ecology: an ethic of interdependence, care, and reverence.

In this context, the practitioner of the Way of the Kami sees themselves not as dominator of the world, but as part of it. Their life is a dance between the visible and the invisible, between daily gesture and deep sacredness. Planting, harvesting, cleaning, preparing a meal—all can be ritual, if done consciously. The world is not dead, nor is it there to be exploited. It is home, it is temple, it is an extension of the spiritual body itself.

By recognizing nature as sacred space and not utilitarian resource, Shinto invites humans to rethink their presence in the world. The spirituality emerging from contact with moss, breeze, moonlight, is not built through rigid rules, but springs from sensitive listening and silent surrender. This form of religiosity is intimate, yet collective; personal, but universal. It is in caring for the surroundings—not stepping on wildflowers, cleaning a dew-covered stone, gently gathering fallen leaves—that the bond between the visible and invisible, between body and spirit, is revealed. Thus, the natural world also becomes an inner mirror, where every living being reflects possibilities of our own way of existing.

This ecological spirituality, born from the encounter between presence and landscape, does not negate the contradictions or pains of existence. On the contrary: it teaches to embrace them with serenity. The mountain housing the kami can also be landslide and storm. The sea cradling contemplation can turn tempest. But even what hurts does not cease to be sacred. In Shinto, the beautiful is not separated from the dangerous, the gentle from the potent—all is manifestation of the force permeating the universe. It is in recognizing this totality that an ethic of humility arises, where humans abandon the arrogance of control and return to the role of caretaker, learner, guest in a living world.

Each season, each cycle of nature, then teaches about balance, impermanence, and rebirth. Being part of the Way of the Kami is accepting nature's invitation to dance to the rhythm of the cosmos. It is allowing the everyday to be pierced by moments of silence and attention, where the spirit can breathe with the world. The spirituality revealed by listening to running water or contemplating the gentle fall of a leaf requires no effort—only presence. In this state, the world reveals its deepest face, and the human being rediscovers their place not at the top, but at the center of a great web of sacred relationships. Thus, living becomes art, and nature, instead of landscape, becomes prayer.

# Chapter 4
# Rites of Purity

The soul of Shinto rests upon a silent yet inflexible principle: purity. No practice, ritual, or true connection with the kami can dispense with it. In the Shinto world, the sacred does not approach what is disordered, murky, dirty, or unbalanced. Approaching the divine is possible only when what is obscured is cleansed. And this cleansing is not restricted to the physical. It extends to energy, mind, spirit. What is sought is a state of clarity, lightness, receptivity. To be pure is to be attuned to the vibration of the gods.

But one must understand what Shinto calls impurity—*kegare*—to grasp the value of purity—*kiyome*. Unlike Western religious conceptions, where moral evil is often associated with sin, voluntary error, or violation of commandments, in Shinto, impurity does not necessarily carry guilt or condemnation. It can be a natural consequence of life. Birth, death, blood, illness, mourning—all these states generate *kegare*. Not because they are evil, but because they disrupt the subtle balance between the visible and invisible worlds.

Impurity is like a mist that accumulates and distances the kami. They do not hate the impure. They simply withdraw before it. Therefore, spiritual life demands constant renewal. Purity is a process, not a fixed state. It is achieved and lost, and must be restored constantly, just as the body is washed each day. Spiritual dirt is inevitable, but also easily washed away, if there is intention and discipline.

Among Shinto's most emblematic practices is *misogi*, the rite of purification with water. Its symbolism is ancestral: water, with its fluidity and capacity to flow, carries away impurities of body and soul. The practitioner bathes in rivers, waterfalls, or even with buckets of cold water, in a gesture that is both physical and spiritual. The body stiffens with cold, the heart concentrates, the mind silences. There is no room for distractions. Every drop that runs off is an offering to the harmony one wishes to restore. *Misogi* requires no grand ceremonies. It can be done alone, in silence, with respect. Some groups perform more intense rituals, with chants, rhythmic breathing, rhythmic clapping that awakens the spirit and prepares the body for immersion. The experience is always profound. The pain of cold gives way to unusual clarity. The spirit awakens. The soul opens.

Another essential rite is *harae*, performed by priests with the aid of symbolic objects, such as the ōnusa (a wand with strips of white paper, called *shide*, hanging from its ends). The priest waves the wand over a person, object, or place, dissipating accumulated impurity. This movement is accompanied by sacred words—*norito*—that invoke the kami of purification and ask for harmony to be restored. *Harae* can be performed in homes, cars, new constructions, work tools. Anything that comes into contact with life can, and should, be purified. In major ceremonies, like seasonal festivals or rites of passage, *harae* is an indispensable part of preparation. It precedes sacred gestures, ensuring the spiritual environment is clean and ready to receive the deities. The shrine must be clean, the priests must be clean, the participants too. It is not just physical hygiene—it is an energetic frequency that must be kept high, smooth, transparent.

But there is also a more subtle purity: the purity of attitude, mind, intention. Living with *kokoro tadashiku*—a correct heart—is a way of keeping the soul pure. Avoiding resentment, acting honestly, respecting others, being grateful for blessings received—all are forms of continuous purification. Anger, envy, arrogance, even if not manifested in acts, obscure the spirit. The Shinto path requires inner vigilance. Not to generate guilt, but to keep the presence of the kami close.

The environment is also a reflection of inner purity. A clean, organized, beautiful space—even if simple—is more than a reflection of aesthetics. It is an invitation to the sacred. Therefore, cleaning the house is also a religious act. One sweeps the floor as one sweeps the soul. One arranges a room as one prepares an altar. Spirituality is lived not only in the temple, but in every gesture made consciously.

In shrines, care for cleanliness is visible and constant. Path stones are washed, fallen leaves gathered, wood polished, objects replaced regularly. The dust of time is not allowed to accumulate. What is sought is the freshness of the present moment. The kami do not inhabit the old and dusty—they move where there is vitality and renewal.

Even in dress, Shinto cultivates purity. Priests wear white garments, symbolizing cleanliness and light. White is not the color of absence, but of fullness. It is the mirror reflecting all tones, the cloth that does not hide, the open space for divine presence. To dress in white in a ritual is to dress in sky.

Food, though not codified with rigid prohibitions, also carries spiritual implications. Eating attentively, giving thanks before and after meals, avoiding excess, respecting food as nature's offering—all keep the body light and the spirit attentive. Food is energy. What enters the body becomes part of the soul. And therefore, one should eat as if performing a rite.

In rites of passage, such as ceremonies for birth, marriage, or coming of age, purification is the first step. One does not cross a threshold without first washing away the residues of the previous cycle. The new stage requires new energy. The baby is purified to enter this world with blessing. The couple is purified to unite their souls in harmony. The youth is purified to walk as an adult. Life, in Shinto, is made of cycles, and each cycle is restarted by cleansing the previous one.

Purity is not a goal. It is a constant process. A daily practice. A way of living. And in this living, the devotee approaches the kami not because they desire favors or rewards, but because they wish to live in consonance with the invisible order of the world. Shinto does not create a moral tribunal—it creates a vibrational field. And in this field, only what is clear, light, and sincere resonates.

The practice of purity requires no isolation. On the contrary, it strengthens through coexistence. Harmony with others, mutual respect, care for common space—all are ways of keeping the atmosphere clean. Purity is not selfish introspection—it is openness to others, to the environment, to the sacred.

Therefore, when someone approaches a shrine, they do not do so as if entering any building. They first pass by the *temizuya*, the water font where hands are washed and the mouth rinsed. It is a simple but profoundly symbolic gesture. The hands, which touch the world, must be clean. The mouth, which speaks words, must be fresh. Body and spirit must be in tune with the sacred place.

Only then does the devotee cross the *torii* and walk towards the *honden*, the heart of the shrine. Crossing the *torii*, after purification, is not just physical movement—it is a change of state. Upon passing this portal, the devotee enters a dimension where time slows, attention sharpens, and the heart quiets. Each step towards the *honden* is a gesture of listening, of silent reverence. There is no need for long words or promises. What is offered is clean presence, a prepared body, a spirit willing to feel. Walking becomes prayer, and the silence between gestures acquires spiritual density. Purity, at this moment, is not just preparation—it is communion.

Shinto teaches that this communion does not end within the shrine's limits. Returning home, the practitioner carries the vibration of the sacred space, like carrying a breeze in the fabric of clothes or a light scent in the hair. The home can be a continuation of the shrine, the street an extension of the sacred path. If the world is inhabited by kami, then everywhere can be a place of purification. A simple bath at day's end, cleaning done calmly, a conversation avoiding rancor—all are acts restoring inner clarity. To live with purity is to live awake, with eyes recognizing the delicacy of the instant.

Purity, therefore, is not an unattainable ideal, nor a rigid requirement. It is a continuous listening to what vibrates within us and around us. An attention that does not judge, but perceives. A practice that does not exclude, but embraces. In the Way of the Kami, being pure is not being perfect—it is being willing to restart, to wash away grievances, to blow away the dust of days. And it is in this delicate movement of daily restoration that the spirit stays alive, and the presence of the gods remains close. Purity is the bridge between the human and the invisible—and as long as there are those who cultivate it, the world will continue to be sacred.

# Chapter 5
# Sacred Spaces

There are places where time slows down. Where the sound of footsteps seems clearer, the wind blows with meaning transcending the physical, and the heart quiets even before understanding why. Such places do not arise by chance. They are prepared, guarded, honored. They are the Shinto shrines—known as *jinja*—spaces where the visible bows before the invisible, and where the presence of the kami reveals itself through form, harmony, and silence.

Each *jinja* is more than a building. It is a spiritual field shaped precisely to welcome deities. Its structure, though physical, materializes an invisible atmosphere that existed before wood, stone, metal. The shrine is born first in spirit, then in matter. And so, choosing the location is not random. Many shrines were erected at the foot of sacred mountains, in clearings of ancient forests, beside rivers singing with ancestral force. The place is recognized before being demarcated. Nature whispers its sacredness, and humans simply listen and mark.

The entrance to a shrine is marked by an unmistakable element: the *torii*. This simple structure, composed of two vertical pillars and two horizontal beams, is not a gate in the functional sense. It does not protect with walls, nor impede physical passage. The *torii* is a symbolic marker. It separates the everyday world from the sacred space. Crossing it is an act of transition—from profane to sacred, noise to silence, dispersion to presence. And therefore, one does not cross the *torii* casually. One walks to the side, avoiding the center, which belongs to the gods. One bows the head slightly. One feels the change.

After the *torii*, the visitor almost always encounters the *temizuya*, the purification font. Ladles or wooden dippers rest there, carefully arranged. With them, the devotee washes hands—first left, then right—and finally rinses the mouth. This is not a hygienic ritual, but a profound symbolic act. The body is prepared for the encounter. Hands, which perform actions; the mouth, which utters words. All must be clean, calm, fresh. Water flows, and with it, carries away distraction, weight, restlessness.

The path to the main hall of the shrine—the *honden*—is always marked by an atmosphere of sobriety and respect. Often lined with stone lanterns, ancient trees, small secondary altars dedicated to other kami. Nothing is excessive. Beauty is restrained, subtle, fluid. And it is precisely in this absence of ostentation that its greatness lies. The shrine does not need to impress. It needs to welcome.

Approaching the *honden*, the devotee finds the *haiden*, the hall of prayers. It is there one bows, claps hands, lowers the head, offers silent prayer. One does not enter the *honden*—it is reserved for priests, internal rites, the dwelling place of the kami. The devotee remains at the entrance, as one acknowledging their place with humility and respect. Proximity to the sacred requires not total penetration, but attunement. And this attunement manifests in gesture, posture, sincere heart.

The *honden*, though inaccessible to direct view, holds within it the sacred object representing the kami: it could be a mirror, a sword, a stone, or even nothing visible. What matters is not the object, but the presence it invokes. The mirror, especially, is frequent. Not by chance. It reflects without judging, without distorting. Looking into a mirror is looking at oneself—and realizing the sacred begins in one's own soul.

The architecture of Shinto shrines follows traditional styles dating back to early times. Styles like *shinmei-zukuri*, *nagare-zukuri*, and *taisha-zukuri* define forms and proportions harmonizing the building with the environment. The use of natural wood, curved roofs covered with cypress bark, precise joinery without nails—all reflect integration with nature, a refusal of artificiality. The temple does not impose itself on the environment—it fits into it. And this constructive harmony extends spiritual harmony.

The shrine environment is maintained with zeal. Paths are swept regularly. Leaves are gathered, but never aggressively. Trees are cared for, not pruned arbitrarily. Stones are washed. Moss is often preserved. Every detail carries the presence of the kami. Nothing is mere scenery. Everything is part of the place's spirit. Even sounds—the tinkling of bells, the echo of claps, the murmur of water—are considered voices of the sacred.

Besides being places of individual worship, shrines serve an essential social function. They are the spiritual heart of communities. Festivals, weddings, seasonal celebrations, blessings for children, inaugurations—all pass through the *jinja*. It is there the people gather, local identity strengthens, the link between past and present reactivates. The protective kami of the village, city, neighborhood—the *ujigami*—is honored there, and its presence ensures protection, fertility, peace.

Children, from an early age, are taken to the shrine. At birth, at ages three, five, and seven (*Shichi-Go-San*), on the first days of the new year. They learn not by imposition, but by immersion. The shrine is part of life. Youth, elders, newlyweds—all maintain a living, affective relationship with the *jinja*. It is not a distant temple, but the community's center of spiritual energy.

Visiting a shrine is not tourism. It is a spiritual gesture. Even if the visitor is foreign, even if they do not know the rites in detail, if there is respect, the kami perceives. What matters is intention. Crossing the *torii* with reverence. Purifying oneself sincerely. Praying with a present heart. It is not necessary to understand everything—it is necessary to feel. And this sensitivity opens the way to divine presence.

These sacred spaces, therefore, do not impose themselves through grandeur, but touch the intimate through the delicacy with which they welcome the invisible. It is in the simplicity of aged wood, the silent geometry of lines, the cool shade under trees that the true dimension of the sacred is revealed. The *jinja* does not aim to be a palace for distant gods, but a home of passage, where divinity and humanity intersect in a moment of harmony. Everything there invites quietude—a quietude that is not absence, but amplified presence. Every detail is an invitation to listen: to the sound of one's own steps, the rustling of leaves, what the slowed heart can finally hear.

This listening deepens further during *matsuri*, Shinto festivals, when the shrine pulses like the community's heart. In these celebrations, the kami symbolically leave the *honden* and are carried in processions, in *mikoshi* (portable shrines), through the city streets. It is the divinity meeting the people, and the people responding with music, dance, offerings, joy. There is no contradiction between the recollection of silence and the clamor of the festival—both are legitimate ways to honor the sacred. The sacred space then expands, overflowing the temple limits to encompass the entire village, all of life. In these moments, the everyday is purified by celebration, and collective memory is reanimated like renewed fire.

Ultimately, the *jinja* remains a tangible link between worlds, a bridge built with reverence, beauty, and humility. It reminds us that the sacred need not be sought on high, but cared for on the ground we tread, in gestures repeated with an awakened soul. Each visit to a shrine is a return to that place where time bends, presence is denser, even the air seems to pray. And when one crosses the *torii* again to leave, something has changed. The world outside is the same—but the one inhabiting it now carries a little more silence in the chest and light in the eyes.

# Chapter 6
# Offerings and Prayers

The universe listens. Even in silence, every vibration emitted by a sincere heart reaches the kami. In Shinto, no intermediaries are necessary between humans and the sacred. There are rites, forms, gestures—but none hold value without what lies at the center of everything: purity of feeling, true intention, *magokoro*. Offerings and prayers are not currency for exchange. They are expressions of gratitude, recognition, reverence. They are ways of saying: 'I am here. I see. I honor.'

Offerings, or *shinsen*, are diverse. They can be white rice, representing essential sustenance given by the earth. Salt, symbol of purification and vital energy. Fresh water, for its fluidity and purifying force. Sake, as a celebration of life. Branches of *sakaki*, the sacred tree whose firm, green leaves never fall. But above all, sincere words—prayer made from the heart—are the most precious offering.

The act of offering follows no rigid model. There is a traditional structure, but within it lives a freedom allowing authentic expression from each practitioner. The gesture of placing a handful of rice, lighting a candle, pouring a few drops of sake, carefully folding paper and depositing it respectfully—all are ritual. All are communication. And thus the bond between human and kami is built.

When a devotee approaches a shrine, they carry not only desires or hopes. They also bring their history, feelings, connections. The shrine welcomes everything. The space is prepared for this. Arriving before the *haiden*, the prayer hall, the faithful performs an ancestral gesture: tosses a small coin into the offering box, rings the bell—if there is one—bows deeply, claps twice, joins hands, and remains silent. Then, bows again. This gesture is known and respected throughout Japan. It needs no explanation—it is understood by the heart.

The two claps are more than applause. They awaken the kami, harmonize the worlds, align human presence with divine vibration. It is a clap that breaks dispersion, concentrates the spirit. The claps echo like the sound of the soul calling the unseen. The initial and final bows frame the sacred moment. Prayer, made in silence, can contain requests, thanks, promises. It can be long or brief. But it must always arise from an authentic inner state. There are no mandatory formulas. The most powerful prayer in Shinto is one that flows naturally, without need for words.

Yet, formal prayers exist—the *norito*—recited on special occasions by priests. *Norito* are archaic texts, written in classical Japanese, revering the kami, narrating devotees' merits, asking for blessings, expressing gratitude. They are intoned with rhythm, intonation, solemnity. Each syllable pronounced with respect. *Norito* is not recited—it is offered. And in this offering, it carries the soul of the ceremony. Unlike mechanically repeated prayers, *norito* do not aim for control. They do not seek to bend the divine to human will. They narrate, tell, share. They are like ceremonial letters. At their center is always recognition: of the human place, the gods' generosity, the world's beauty. Asking comes later. First, one recognizes.

Besides words, there are also symbolic forms of offering. *Tamagushi*, *sakaki* branches decorated with white paper strips, are presented in many ceremonies. The gesture of offering them follows a precise ritual: the branch is held with both hands, slowly rotated, raised to face level, and placed before the altar. Each movement is charged with meaning. There is no rush. The kami's time is different. And the devotee, when offering, must abandon their urgencies.

In many homes, even far from shrines, there are small domestic altars—*kamidana*—where daily offerings are also made. Fresh water at dawn. Freshly cooked rice. Green sprigs. Words of thanks. Respectful silences. This daily practice extends the shrine. The home also becomes sacred space. The everyday, then, is experienced with a different gaze. Each meal is a gift. Each morning, a blessing. The kami is there, not above, but beside.

During festivals or difficult times, devotees write wishes on small wooden plaques called *ema*, decorated with images and symbols. These plaques are hung on structures near the shrine. Reading the requests reveals the essence of the human spirit: health, peace, protection, success, harmony. But there is also gratitude. Many *ema* are messages of thanks for granted wishes, healings, reunions. The kami are not just sources of power. They are invisible companions walking alongside those who live sincerely.

Throughout the year, there are also collective offering rituals. Large tables are set before altars with rice, fruits, fish, vegetables, sweets. All fresh, beautiful, arranged harmoniously. It is not about feeding the gods—they do not nourish themselves like humans. But about expressing, through abundance and care, respect for all that has been received. Offering is also returning. What comes from the earth returns to the earth. What is gift, is shared.

Offerings and prayers, thus, are not isolated actions. They are part of a sacred ethic. They teach to thank before asking. To recognize before desiring. To quiet before acting. Shinto does not worry about specific faith content, but about the posture with which one lives. The act of offering, however simple, if performed with *magokoro*, is complete. The gesture without sincerity, however elaborate, remains empty.

Therefore, in shrines, even priests bow humbly. They do not position themselves as superior to devotees, but as servants of the kami. Their role is to care for rites, tend spaces, keep the bridge open. They recite, prepare, clean, teach. But the link with the kami belongs to each individual. There is no intercession. There is communion.

Faced with all this, it is clear Shinto spirituality requires no grand demonstrations. It requires truth. A candle lit with attention. A branch placed respectfully. A whispered thanks at sunset. All this is worship. All this is offering. And when the heart is full, the kami listens. Not with ears, but with presence. And in this invisible encounter between human and divine, the entire world harmonizes.

Shinto practice reveals, in its essence, a delicate pedagogy of the sacred that educates the gaze to the beauty of small things. More than following precepts, it is a daily exercise in perception—perceiving the sacredness insinuating itself in the steam of freshly cooked rice, the gleam of offered fresh water, the silence preceding prayer. This inner education transforms not only the religious act but the very way of being in the world. Offering, in this context, is not a rite separate from life, but life transfigured into rite. It is when everyday existence rises to the dimension of mystery and becomes language understandable by the kami.

This silent, attentive spirituality also teaches the value of presence. In the kami's time, everything happens slowly. Gesture needs pause, thought needs clarity, heart needs truth. This sacred slowness opposes the rush of the modern world and, in this contrast, offers healing. Each prayer, each offered branch, each *ema* hung in shrines reveals a way to slow down and find the center. By recognizing sacredness in the simple, the faithful transforms the space around them and, even more, themselves. It is this recognition that makes each offering an act of communion, not separation—a gesture of reconnection with nature, with others, and with the unseen.

Ultimately, the image remains of a world where the sacred need not be invoked by grand words, but merely awakened by a true gesture. It is in the reverent everyday, in the simplicity of ritual lived consciously, that the encounter with the kami manifests. Shinto invites us to this listening: to live with a heart that perceives, hands that thank, and a spirit that recognizes. For where *magokoro* exists, even silence becomes prayer, and even the lightest breath of wind can carry an offering.

# Chapter 7
# Seasonal Festivals

There are moments when time does not pass—it spins. The wheel of seasons, with its colors, sounds, and scents, marks more than climatic changes: it is the rhythm of life itself. In Shinto, this turning is not ignored, nor confronted—it is celebrated. And each cycle completed is an invitation to spiritual renewal. *Matsuri*, the seasonal festivals, are the living expression of this communion with the world's natural rhythm and the constant presence of the kami. They are not just folkloric events or cultural manifestations—they are sacred rituals reaffirming the link between heaven, earth, and community.

Festivals are born of earth and time. Each season carries its own vibration, a distinct spirit, and *matsuri* are its ceremonial language. Winter invites introspection and withdrawal; spring, renewal and blossoming; summer, fullness and vitality; autumn, harvest and gratitude. And the gods, as active parts of these cycles, are called to participate in the celebration, to bless fields, families, homes, and hearts.

The most celebrated of all festivals is *Shōgatsu*, the Japanese New Year. More than a chronological turn, it is an energetic transition. The days preceding

*Shōgatsu* are dedicated to purifying homes, paying debts, reconciling with relatives and friends. Everything must be renewed, for the year's kami—the *Toshigami*—comes to visit each home. Doors are adorned with *shimenawa*, rice straw ropes warding off *kegare*, and entrances with *kadomatsu*, pine and bamboo arrangements welcoming the visiting spirit. The year's first shrine visit—*hatsumōde*—is a collective gesture of prayer and hope. Millions travel, face the cold, wait long hours in silence to make offerings, clap hands, express gratitude. A new cycle begins, and the first gesture must be reverence.

At winter's end, *Setsubun* is celebrated, the ritual transition to spring. On this day, accumulated impurities must be expelled from home and spirit. It is time to shout: '*Oni wa soto! Fuku wa uchi!*'—'Demons out! Luck in!'—while throwing roasted soybeans out of the house. This seemingly simple gesture carries intense symbolic force. The 'demons' represent all that obscures the soul: grievances, fears, resentments, illnesses. Expelling them is more than theater. It is an act of spiritual courage. In temples and shrines, priests and special guests perform the same gesture on a larger scale, with crowds gathered to share in collective purification.

Spring's arrival is marked by flower festivals, like *Hanami*, where contemplating cherry blossoms becomes a national rite. Families gather under trees, picnic, share stories, sing. But something subtler happens: under flowers soon to fall, people reconcile with ephemerality. Beauty lasting briefly becomes precious. And thus,

Shinto spirituality—seeing the divine in the transient—manifests in the joy of gatherings, reverence for nature, silence between laughs.

Summer brings the most vibrant *matsuri*. Streets fill with color, music, movement. Lanterns are lit, food stalls erected, and *mikoshi*—small portable shrines—are carried by groups of men and women in ceremonial attire. The *mikoshi* is not a mere replica. It carries the spirit of the shrine's kami, processing through streets to visit the community, bless homes, renew bonds. The sound of drums, rhythmic shouts of bearers, summer heat—all merge into a cosmic dance. The kami, at this moment, is not just on the altar—it walks among the people, participates in the festival, observes faces, receives enthusiasm as offering.

Among many summer festivals, *Tanabata* stands out, inspired by the legend of two stellar lovers separated by the Milky Way, meeting only once a year. During *Tanabata*, children and adults write wishes on colorful paper strips, hung on bamboo branches. These wishes are not just individual hopes—they are expressions of collective spirit, voices rising to the heavens like multicolored prayers. Bamboo, with its flexibility and strength, supports the unseen. And the wind passing through the papers is heard by the gods.

Autumn is the harvest season, bringing festivals of gifts. The most symbolic is *Niiname-sai*, celebrated by the emperor in thanks for the new rice harvest. Rice in Japan is more than food—it is offering, energy, life. Cultivating it is a spiritual act. Harvesting it, a blessing. Sharing it, a celebration. In *Niiname-sai*, the emperor offers freshly harvested rice to the gods, in ceremonial robes and restrained gestures, in a rite linking the people's heart to earth and sky. In rural communities, harvest festivals are lived intensely. Offerings are taken to local shrines. Children participate with traditional dances. Lion masks, puppets, folk music—all unite in an expression of joy and reverence. There is no separation between spiritual and everyday. The farmer who plants and harvests also prays and gives thanks. Food, before consumption, is symbolically returned to the kami who made it possible.

*Matsuri*, though diverse in form, share a common spirit: celebrating life in all its phases. They are not just cultural memory—they are living spiritual practices. Joy is not seen as dispersion, but intense presence. Dancing, singing, eating, dressing carefully—all are offerings. And so, in Shinto festivals, beauty is cultivated. Clothes are special. Hair is arranged. Movements follow ancestral patterns. The body becomes instrument of the sacred.

Participating in a festival, the devotee not only honors the kami—they reconnect with their own essence. They remember being part of a community, a landscape, an eternal cycle of transformation. The collective spirit forming in *matsuri* reinforces feelings of belonging, unity, harmony. And even those arriving as visitors, if open-hearted, feel this field. They are welcomed not by doctrines, but by gestures. And in these gestures, find an invitation: live with more presence, reverence, joy.

Amidst the splendor of *matsuri*, one of Shinto spirituality's deepest lessons is revealed: sacredness lies not only in moments of silence and contemplation, but also in the vibration of life in its fullness. When the kami descend to walk among devotees, there is no separation between divine and human—there is fusion. The dance of bodies, gleam of lanterns, crowd's warmth are expressions of the same impulse moving nature through seasons. Participating in a festival is participating in existence's own flow, where each drumbeat calls to consciousness, and each wish hung in the wind bridges worlds.

*Matsuri*'s cyclical presence also teaches that time is not a river running straight, but a living field where everything returns in another form, color, flavor. Festivals are not repetitions—they are rebirths. The same offering gains new meaning each season, for the heart offering it is no longer the same. There is silent maturation happening when time is lived reverently: one learns to embrace cold and heat, flower and fallen leaf, beginning and end. And so, spirituality emerging from festivals is made not just of faith, but deep learning from life's own rhythm.

Ultimately, what remains is not just memory of colors or chants, but the feeling of having touched something larger than oneself. In *matsuri*, humans perceive themselves part of an invisible network uniting earth, sky, and hearts. This perception transforms: it awakens care, strengthens community bonds, reignites the inner spark seeking meaning. And when the festival ends, the kami returns to the shrine, but something of it remains—in the home's silence, the firmness of daily gestures, the renewed gaze learning to see, in each season, a new chance to celebrate life.

# Chapter 8
# Protector Gods

In the Shinto universe, there is no single throne where a central, absolute deity rests. There is no supreme, distant, immutable god. Instead, there is a myriad of presences. Spirits, forces, consciousnesses—the kami—inhabiting the world, manifesting in infinite forms, sharing a dynamic existence with humans. Shinto protector gods are not abstract figures or untouchable archetypes. They are close. Present. They act in communities, families, trees, crafts, emotions. The world, to reverent eyes, is inhabited by thousands of kami.

Among this vast spiritual constellation, *ujigami* hold a special place. They are the protector kami of clans, villages, neighborhoods, or entire cities. Each traditional community has its own. It is not just a symbol—it is a member of the community. Prayers are directed to it in times of illness, drought, harvest, celebration. Its presence is not decorative, but operative. The *ujigami* protects, observes, responds. And each shrine dedicated to it becomes that people's spiritual heart. In these places, seasonal festivals, rites of passage, collective celebrations are not just religious events—they are reunions with the invisible guardian sharing the common destiny.

Besides *ujigami*, kami exist associated with specific aspects of human life. These are gods not merely representing ideas, but acting in concrete spheres. Inari Ōkami, for example, is one of the most popular and multifaceted. His image is associated with rice, fertility, agriculture, business, prosperity. Shrines dedicated to Inari are easily recognizable by the rows of red *torii* multiplying like a flaming tunnel between worlds. His messengers are white foxes—*kitsune*—appearing in pairs at shrine entrances, often with rice keys in their mouths. Inari is invoked by farmers, merchants, students, and all wishing to prosper in their endeavors. But more than bringing fortune, he teaches respect for the harvest cycle, sharing fruits, always giving thanks.

Another kami of great devotion is Hachiman, god of war, but not in the Western warlike sense. Hachiman protects warriors, yes, but also communities, fishermen, and especially peace. He is the nation's guardian and the ancestral spirit of Emperor Ōjin, deified after death. His shrines spread across Japan, his presence associated with strength, protection, loyalty. Hachiman is not a distant god, but a spirit responding to the moment's need, whether in battle, sea crossing, or protecting a sick child.

Tenjin, in turn, is the kami of studies and arts. His human name was Sugawara no Michizane, a Heian period scholar and poet who, unjustly exiled, died broken-hearted. After his death, supernatural events frightened the capital, and he was recognized as kami and honored with temples to appease his wrath and restore harmony. Today, Tenjin is revered by students of all ages. During exam times, his shrines fill with youths holding notebooks, depositing *ema* with prayers, asking for concentration, luck, wisdom. He is a god who knows the pain of injustice, but offers light to those seeking knowledge sincerely.

Other kami are associated with health, maternity, longevity, fertility, art. Konohanasakuya-hime, goddess of flowers and volcanoes, is invoked by pregnant women. Sarutahiko Ōkami, with his long face and robust strength, is a god of paths and encounters, protector of travelers and difficult decisions. Ame-no-Uzume, goddess of dance and laughter, is celebrated as the one who awakened the world's light and continues to cheer souls with her sacred irreverence. And there are many others, with forgotten names and silent functions, inhabiting small altars, hidden forests, humble homes. None is lesser. All have their unique strength and face.

The relationship with protector gods is built through practice and intimacy. The devotee not only knows names—they coexist. Visits the shrine, offers prayers, participates in festivals, recognizes signs. A kami might be invoked for generations in the same family, the relationship becoming a link between ancestors and descendants. The domestic altar, the *kamidana*, is often consecrated to a specific kami whose energy resonates with the family's vocation: protector of agriculture, fishing, writing, health, carpentry.

This personal connection with kami does not prevent revering others. Shinto requires no exclusivity. A practitioner can, and often does, visit different shrines, honor different gods, ask protection in various life areas. Each kami is a specific focus of cosmic energy. And humans, multifaceted as they are, can connect to multiple presences according to spiritual need. It is common, even, to adopt a kami as personal protector, not by imposition, but affinity. Sometimes this choice is intuitive—a shrine touching the soul, a name emerging in difficult times, a dream bringing a specific figure. Kami communicate through signs, synchronicities, feelings. One living attentively to details, respecting small gestures and moments of silence, learns to recognize this communication. And then, the bond deepens.

The presence of protector gods is not a guarantee of absence of difficulties. But it is certainty of companionship. When lighting a candle, offering a sprig of fresh leaves, clapping before a small wooden altar, one is saying: 'I do not walk alone.' And this awareness transforms living. Brings serenity amidst chaos. Inspires courage facing the uncertain. Sustains the soul in days of shadow.

Therefore, knowing protector gods is also knowing oneself. Because each kami resonates with a part of human experience. Susanoo's wrath, Amaterasu's brilliance, Izanami's sacrifice, Takamimusubi's wisdom—all inhabit the soul's fabric. They are not outside. They are alongside. And recognizing them, revering them, dialoguing with them is rediscovering the path of harmony.

Shinto protector gods, reflecting multiple aspects of nature and the human soul, reveal a profoundly integrative spirituality. Each kami is simultaneously natural force and affective presence, living archetype and close companion. Walking through a grove, crossing a shrine's red gates, or even silencing before the small domestic altar, the devotee recognizes their journey is accompanied by invisible intelligences demanding not blind worship, but respect and presence. This constant coexistence with the sacred teaches that protection comes not from power imposed from outside, but from a bond built over time, with repeated gestures, with sensitive listening to life.

This bond, however, is not limited to the individual. It extends to community, landscape, craft, past, future. When a family reveres the same kami for generations, the altar ceases to be object: it becomes meeting point between times and affections. When a neighborhood gathers to celebrate the local kami, it is not just asking protection—it is reaffirming collective identity. And thus Shinto intertwines spiritual with social, mystical with everyday. Protector gods do not hover distantly in unreachable spheres: they lean over rooftops, accompany writing a letter, guard children's sleep, sit invisibly at the table when rice is served.

Ultimately, more than seeking gods' favor, the practitioner transforms into the very expression of respect felt for them. Offering, prayer, care for the altar are reflections of an inner posture learning to walk with humility and attention. Kami protect, yes, but also teach—to see beauty in simplicity, honor the ancient, embrace the mutable. And so, living under Shinto gods' protection is, fundamentally, living consciously: of self, other, nature, and the mystery permeating all things.

# Chapter 9
# The Home Altar

In the silence of an ordinary morning, before the day's noises settle in, a simple gesture repeats in many Japanese homes: lighting a candle, offering fresh water, bowing in reverence before a small wooden altar. This practice, devoid of fanfare or spectacle, is the essence of Shinto worship lived daily. The name of this altar is *kamidana*—literally, 'god shelf'—and its discreet presence sustains, like an invisible column, the home's spirituality.

The *kamidana* is not a symbol. It is a direct point of contact between the visible and invisible. A permanent link with the kami. It is not a miniature temple or decorative object. It is, in itself, a sacred space. An extension of the shrine, adapted to domestic life's rhythm. And its presence transforms the home into a temple, not by grandeur, but by the pure intention with which it is cared for and revered.

Placing a *kamidana* at home is an act of spiritual choice. It requires no priesthood, no Japanese birth, no adherence to rigid rules. What is demanded is respect, sincerity, constancy. The altar should be installed in a high, clean place, easily reached by gaze, but where the body does not touch it inadvertently. Preferably facing south or east—directions associated with light and rebirth. Never above an entrance or bathroom, and never below any structure. The kami deserves to be above, not by hierarchy, but honor.

The heart of the *kamidana* is the *ofuda*—a sacred talisman received from a shrine, containing the name of the kami venerated there. This *ofuda* is the spiritual presence of the god in question. It consecrates the space. And therefore, must be treated with the same care one would show the real presence of a divine guest. Around it, small ritual objects can be arranged: two small containers for water and sake, two for rice and salt, a vase for *sakaki* branches, candles, and incense. Simplicity is the rule. But each item, however discreet, carries function and meaning.

Offerings at the *kamidana* are performed similarly to those at shrines. Clean water every morning, changed before dawn. Fresh rice on special dates or after main meals. Green sprigs representing life, renewal, connection. Abundance is not necessary—enough that it is pure, fresh, honest. And most importantly: accompanied by a sincere heart, the *magokoro*. Because the offering's value is not material, but the vibration it transmits.

Before the altar, the devotee performs the same traditional gesture: two bows, two claps, silent prayer, and a final bow. This small ritual, repeated daily, restructures the spirit. It reorders attention, undoes anxiety's knots, realigns being with life's flow. And so, the *kamidana* is not just a prayer point—it is a mirror of the soul. It reflects the inner state of its keeper. If neglected, dusty, ignored, something breaks in the bond with the gods. The kami does not abandon—but falls silent.

Many practitioners feel the direct effect of cultivating this space. The home's atmosphere changes. Becomes lighter, quieter, more orderly. Conflicts lessen. Decisions gain clarity. Life, though challenges remain, seems to flow more smoothly. Because the home ceases to be just physical shelter and becomes abode of spirituality.

There is no single type of kami that can be honored on the domestic altar. Most common is consecrating the *kamidana* to the kami of the nearest shrine or the deity with whom the family has historical or affective ties. One can also include more than one *ofuda*, provided the space is expanded respectfully. Inari, for example, is often honored in homes linked to agriculture, business, or cooking. Tenjin appears in students' homes. Amaterasu, as sun goddess and ancestor of harmony, is welcome in any home. But essential is that the choice is made consciously and with affinity. The kami should be treated as a beloved guest, staying home every day.

The *kamidana* is also a point of family union. Parents, children, grandparents can share this prayer space. Teaching children to care for the altar transmits not just rite, but worldview. It teaches there is something beyond the visible, gratitude must be cultivated, beauty of small things has value. The child offering water to the kami learns, without words, that living is a gift, and this gift must be honored.

On celebration days, the *kamidana* gains new elements. Small sweets, seasonal fruits, fresh flowers, handwritten messages. One can sing, dance before it, as ways to gladden the kami. There is no rigidity. There is life. And this life is spiritualized by gesture, intention, conscious repetition. Repetition not as blind habit, but rhythm generating stability.

If by chance the *ofuda* becomes old, damaged, or completes an annual cycle, it should be returned to its shrine of origin, where it will be burned in appropriate ceremony. A new *ofuda* is then received, renewing the pact with the kami, like renewing vows of invisible friendship. This simple gesture reinforces Shinto's cyclical nature—everything is born, fulfills its time, returns to the invisible. And the devotee, participating in this cycle, also becomes part of the eternal dance between the world and the gods.

No need to wait for special occasions to pray at the *kamidana*. It is always there, silent witness to the daily journey. Leaving home for work, a bow. Returning, thanks. Before an important decision, a short prayer. Achieving a goal, an offering of gratitude. Shinto spirituality is made of simple gestures, integrated into life's rhythm. And the domestic altar is the anchor sustaining this integration.

The *kamidana* teaches the divine is not just in distant temples, sacred mountains, grand rituals. It is in the living room, kitchen, bedroom corner. It is in how the house is arranged, others cared for, food prepared. The home, when inhabited reverently, transforms. And in this transformed space, the kami remain. Therefore, the *kamidana* is not just furniture, nor isolated sacred object. It is a constant reminder of divine presence in the ordinary. It invites attention, cleanliness, gratitude. And by keeping this small altar lit with daily gestures, the devotee not only honors gods—they re-educate themselves. Learns to see with new eyes. To hear silence. To walk more lightly.

By maintaining the daily gesture before the *kamidana*, the practitioner develops spirituality relying not on spectacles, but constancy and presence. This fidelity to small ritual shapes rare sensitivity: ability to recognize sacred in the everyday. It's not about waiting for visible miracles, but cultivating subtle coexistence with the invisible. Over time, this relationship deepens—not by obligation, but affinity. The altar, previously external element, becomes mirror of a quieter, more awake inner world, where each offering is also conversation with one's own soul.

This spiritual silence promoted by *kamidana* has profound implications. It realigns not just the individual, but the home's very atmosphere. Small emotional disorders dissolve. Time seems to slow. Words gain more weight, affections more clarity. And when difficulties arrive—as they inevitably do—there, in that sacred corner of the house, is a place of refuge, a point of balance. The altar responds not with promises, but offers constant remembrance: one is not alone. The kami's presence, even invisible, anchors the heart, sustains the step. This transforms spirituality into something tangible, practicable, accessible anytime.

Ultimately, *kamidana* is less altar, more way of living. It teaches, daily, that the divine is not separate from existence, but intertwined with it. Lighting a candle or renewing water, the devotee not only performs rite—they reaffirm their place in the world, connection with nature, ancestors, life's very essence. And thus, even on an ordinary morning, before day's noises settle, that simple gesture transforms into portal: an instant where human and sacred mutually recognize each other.

# Chapter 10
# Everyday Religion

Shinto spirituality dwells not only in shrines, festivals, formal rites. It requires no ceremonial robes, ancient words, complex ceremonies to manifest. It lives, primarily, in the ordinary. In small gestures and silences. In each greeting, each cleaning done with intention, each meal shared respectfully. Everyday religion in Shinto is continuous practice, almost invisible, but profoundly transformative. It is life lived reverently.

The day's first act, opening eyes, is already encounter with the sacred. The sun rising on the horizon is not just star—it is living light of Amaterasu-ōmikami, the sun goddess. Turning east, even briefly, bowing head slightly in silence recognizes this presence. Many practitioners maintain habit of greeting new day with gesture of gratitude. No fixed words. Just feeling the day beginning is gift, renewal, invitation.

Before meals, the custom of saying '*Itadakimasu*'—literally, 'I humbly receive'—carries deep spiritual meaning. Not just politeness or courtesy. It recognizes food comes from sacred cycle: earth, water, human dedication, gods' blessing. Eating is not mechanical act. It is gesture of communion with elements sustaining life. After the meal, '*Gochisōsama deshita'*—'it was a feast,' even if simple—expresses gratitude not just for food, but all work and energy involved in obtaining it.

Cleaning, in Shinto, is also spiritual practice. The living environment is not just functional space—it is extension of the soul. So, sweeping the house, arranging objects, cleaning floor, airing rooms are not just domestic tasks. They are gestures purifying space and, with it, spirit. Dust accumulating on things differs not from that settling on mind. External order reflects internal harmony. And keeping home clean keeps spirit aligned with kami.

Schools in Japan, profoundly influenced by Shinto spirit, reflect this spiritual discipline. Children learn, early on, to clean classrooms, bathrooms, hallways. No school janitors. Not for economy, but ethical education. Each student becomes responsible for their environment. Learns caring for common space is part of character cultivation. That beauty and order are not just aesthetic, but expressions of respect. This practice, repeated daily, molds the gaze. Teaches seeing world with attention. And this attention is, essentially, form of prayer.

In public transport, lines, streets, silence and courtesy arise not just from social rules. They are also reflections of spirituality recognizing others as sacred presence. Each person carries divine spark. Treating others kindly also honors kami living in all beings. Respectful behavior is not social mask. It is rooted spiritual practice.

Words, in Shinto, are also paths. Speaking sincerely, avoiding gossip, choosing silence when needed—all part of daily practice. The concept of *kotodama*, the 'spirit of words,' reveals belief each sound carries spiritual vibration. Saying something launches energy into world. So, one speaks carefully. Negative words, impulsively uttered, cloud environment. Beautiful words, spoken truly, purify.

Even formal rituals translate into simple daily actions. Starting new task, many bow slightly before workspace. Opening new project, light candle. Before trip, offer brief prayer. These gestures, though discreet, create attention field. And this attention transforms ordinary into extraordinary.

Shinto religiosity separates life not into compartments. Work time, family time, meal time, rest time—all moments of possible encounter with sacred. This form of spirituality imposes not. It insinuates. Roots itself in routine, customs, way of inhabiting world. And so, even those not declaring themselves religious end up practicing Shinto in gestures. Respect for public space, care for aesthetics, silence in natural places, spontaneous reverence before ancient tree—all born from soul shaped by centuries of coexistence with kami.

The practice of *omiyamairi*—baby's first shrine visit—marks, early on, child's insertion into sacred field. Presented to local kami, receives protection, blessed. Gesture not just symbolic. Inaugurates relationship. And even if later in life individual drifts from formal rites, this connection remains latent, silent, alive.

In business, many Japanese companies start year with collective shrine visit. Employees, directors, collaborators gather before altar, make offerings, ask wisdom, protection, harmony. Ritual uniting spirituality and work, recognizing kami as partner in human activities. And this practice echoes in corporate values: dedication, integrity, cooperation. Professional environment, crossed by this spirit, also becomes place of inner cultivation.

In fields, farmers maintain small altars amidst crops. Honor gods of earth, rain, sun. Plant not without praying. Harvest not without thanking. Agriculture, in this context, not just technique. Spiritual art. Each season brings lesson. Waiting, care, patience, accepting impermanence—all form character. And food born from this spiritualized earth carries force beyond physical.

In urban life, even amidst concrete and technology, Shinto spirit finds space. Small shrines between skyscrapers, preserved trees on busy corners, purification fountains in unexpected places—all reminders. Kami requires not untouched nature. Manifests where respect exists. And even hastiest passerby, bowing head passing *torii*, participates in sacred.

Shinto, offering this everyday religiosity, reveals essential lies not in complexity, but consciousness. No separation between life and spirituality. Living well is practicing well. And practicing well is living with beauty, respect, order, gratitude. Need not isolate from world, nor wait for grand occasions. Now is temple. Home is altar. Action is prayer.

Recognizing everyday as sacred space, Shinto invites us to a form of religiosity that imposes not as doctrine, but reveals as lifestyle. This way of sacred living depends not on grand discourses or mystical revelations: builds itself in intimacy of common days. How one walks street, greets someone, touches object carefully. Each gesture becomes spiritual signature, trace of attention which, repeated over time, molds spirit delicately, profoundly. Spirituality separating not profane from sacred—but intertwining them, until indistinguishable.

This awareness transforms gaze. City ceases chaotic space, becomes field of living relations. Daily work converts into expression of purpose. Encounters, even briefest, carry possibility of reverence. And thus, practitioner's spirit rests on solid base: care. Caring for space, word, time, relations. Everyday Shinto is, above all, ethic of care. And this ethic, even silent, profoundly contagious. Needs not be taught by imposition. Transmits by coexistence, like incense aroma remaining after smoke dissipates.

Ultimately, living by this spirituality is daily choice—choice to see beauty where distracted gaze sees only routine. Awakening to subtle dimension crossing existence, denying not pains or difficulties, but seeing in them also kami presence. For if each instant is temple, each action prayer, then living reverently is, itself, sacred path. And on this path, where each step is presence, divine walks alongside—not above, not beyond, but beside, in exact rhythm of life lived with intention.

# Chapter 11
# Roles of the Priest

In a silent shrine, where the air seems lighter and time rests slowly, a figure moves with ceremonial grace. Dressed in white and blue, or perhaps deep red, he walks between the *torii* and the *honden* as if tracing invisible bridges between worlds. He does not impose, does not stand out, does not demand. He serves. This is the *kannushi*, the Shinto priest. His role is not one of spiritual domination, nor exclusive mediation. He is not the owner of the sacred—he is its guardian. And his presence is both discreet and essential.

The *kannushi* is the caretaker of purity, the maintainer of the ritual space's harmony. He does not command the kami. He prepares the ground for them to manifest. He tends the shrine with dedicated hands, preserves the rites with exactitude, intones the *norito* with the voice of tradition. His responsibility is to keep alive the flow between the visible and the invisible, between humans and the gods. His function is not interpretive, but ritual. He does not preach. He acts.

The path to becoming a priest in Shinto does not involve a divine call or individual enlightenment. It involves training, practice, and above all, humility. Many priestly lineages are hereditary, maintained by families who have cared for the same shrines for centuries. But there are also those who train in specific institutions, such as Kokugakuin University or Kogakkan University, where they study history, classical Japanese language, rituals, myths, etiquette, and the priestly way of life. The training is not just technical—it is an immersion in Shinto sensitivity.

The *kannushi's* vestments are part of his symbolic role. The *jōe*, a white linen or silk tunic, represents purity. The *eboshi*, a black cap worn on the head, connects him to the courtly attire of antiquity, reinforcing the solemnity of his presence. In more formal ceremonies, he wears the *sokutai*, a complex set of colorful robes reminiscent of imperial court dress. But even under so many layers, what shines through is lightness. The priest should not draw attention to himself, but channel the presence of the sacred with discretion.

In his hands, he may hold the *ōnusa*, a wooden wand with long strips of white paper—the *shide*—that flutter like waves in the wind. With it, he performs purification. The sound of the strips cutting through the air is not noise—it is vibration. With the *ōnusa*, the priest cleanses the environment, objects, people. Not with imposition, but with ceremonial delicacy. Each movement carries intention. Each gesture, meaning.

The *kannushi* are not isolated. They work in partnership with the *miko*, female ritual assistants, usually young women who serve in shrines wearing white robes and red skirts. The *miko's* presence is luminous and silent. She prepares offerings, performs ceremonial dances—the *kagura*—cares for the aesthetics of the sacred space. Her figure is the living continuity of ancestral shamans, women who, since time immemorial, served as mediums between the kami and humans. The *miko* is not subordinate—she is complementary. Her dance is not entertainment—it is invocation. Her silence is not absence—it is listening.

Together, *kannushi* and *miko* sustain the integrity of the shrine. They are the caretakers of the sacred rhythm. They do not impose moral rules, nor claim ownership of truths. They maintain the flow. They wake early to clean the premises, prepare offerings precisely, recite *norito* in ceremonies of blessing, purification, celebration. They do not place themselves between the devotee and the kami—they simply ensure that space, time, and gesture are ready for the encounter.

In moments of transition in devotees' lives, priests assume a fundamental role. At a child's birth, they perform the *omiyamairi*, the first shrine visit. At weddings, they conduct the *shinzen kekkon*, where the couple vows union before the gods, shares sacred sake, and bows together. In rites of passage from childhood to youth, they are present, guiding with sobriety and tenderness. Each rite conducted by the *kannushi* is an invisible seam in the fabric of life, uniting human experience with the realm of the gods.

But it's not just celebrations. In times of crisis, the priest also acts. Facing natural disasters like earthquakes or typhoons, he performs rituals to restore order, comfort the bereaved, purify the land. His presence becomes an anchor. There are no promises of explanation. There is only the certainty that the kami remains present, and that harmony, even broken, can be restored with sincerity, care, and rites.

Many *kannushi* live alongside the shrines, in attached residences. Their life is simple, marked by the rhythm of days and seasons. They seek no prominence, sell no miracles. Their reward is in service. By caring for the altar, they are caring for the people's soul. By lighting a candle, they are illuminating the path of those who approach. By intoning a *norito*, they are offering their voice as a bridge between worlds. And all this is done with the silence of those who know the essential needs no words.

To be a priest in Shinto is not to wear an identity—it is to sustain a way of being. It is to remain pure, attentive, available. It is to live with the kami, for them, and through them. And therefore, the *kannushi* becomes, himself, a reflection of what he preserves. His posture, his gaze, his gesture, all convey the presence he honors. He is a living symbol of the principle that the sacred is not distant—it is cultivated, cared for, nourished with discrete and continuous actions.

In modern times, many priests face new challenges. The decline of regular practitioners, urbanization, the modernization of language. And yet, they remain steadfast. They adapt, without losing the essence. They welcome foreign visitors with hospitality. They explain rituals patiently. They open the shrine gates to those seeking something—even if they don't know exactly what. Shinto priesthood does not close doors—it keeps them open. Because the kami's presence depends not on nationality, origin, or knowledge. It depends only on sincerity.

At the end of the day, when the lanterns are lit, when the shrine sinks into silence, the priest is still there. Perhaps sweeping the floor with a simple broom. Perhaps cleaning the altar objects. Perhaps sitting silently before the *honden*. No one sees him, no one applauds him. But the kami knows. And that awareness is enough.

Under the soft light of the lanterns, the *kannushi* continues his journey like one walking between worlds, carrying the invisible task of sustaining the bond between the human and the divine. Even as contemporary eyes grow accustomed to noise and speed, there is a silent strength in the repeated gesture, the meticulously executed rite, the care that seeks no recognition. The priest does not distance himself from the present—he embraces it in his own way, showing that even in a constantly changing world, there is space for what endures, for what is cared for in silence. His permanence is resistance, but also compassion.

That is why the *kannushi* represents not only the living memory of a tradition but also its discreet renewal. He welcomes transformations without being distorted by them. If the flow of visitors changes, he changes the way he receives. If language alters, he finds new ways to express the same spirit. Priesthood, thus, reveals itself as a craft of time—a time measured not just by clocks, but by seasons, rites, gestures. And each gesture, even the simplest, still carries the weight and lightness of the sacred.

At the day's final turn, when the incense has dissipated and the night wind caresses the shrine's branches, the *kannushi* remains. Not because he must, but because he chose to be. He does not expect to be remembered—he simply does what must be done. And in this continuous, discreet, committed doing, he dissolves into the office he embraced, like water nourishing the root without drawing attention to itself. It is in disappearing into the gesture that the priest reveals himself whole.

# Chapter 12
# Female Priesthood

In ancient times, when the world was not yet divided by rigid structures of power and spirituality walked in consonance with instinct and intuition, the voices of women echoed in rituals like primordial sound. They danced, chanted songs, interpreted the invisible signs of wind, water, fire. In ancestral Japan, even before Shinto took official forms, female priesthood already existed as a natural expression of spiritual sensitivity. Woman, with her organic connection to life cycles, to the earth, and to the waters of the womb, was a direct channel to the kami.

This link was never lost. It survived time, reforms, masculine structures, political adaptations. It remains, subtle and firm, in the figures of the *miko*—the female spiritual assistants of Shinto shrines—and, more recently, in fully ordained priestesses. Shinto spirituality sees no conflict between the feminine and the sacred. On the contrary, it recognizes in feminine energy an essential expression of the divine.

The figure of the *miko* dates back to ancient shamans, known as *kannagi*, women who received the gods into their bodies, who danced in trance states, who communicated the kami's messages to the people. The most emblematic of these figures is Himiko, the shaman queen who ruled the kingdom of Yamatai in the 3rd century. She did not just command politically—she was the living bridge between worlds. Her authority was spiritual, recognized even in Chinese records. She isolated herself, lived in chastity, and spoke for the gods. Her existence proves that female priesthood is not a modern concession—it is an archaic foundation.

Over time, the figure of the *miko* became institutionalized, but without losing its ritual character. She became the guardian of ceremonial beauty, sacred dance, silent offering. Dressed in white and red, with long sleeves and gentle movements, she moves through the sacred space like a presence without weight, like wind reorganizing the place's energy. Her dance—the *kagura*—is not performance. It is invocation. Each gesture is a word. Each turn, a greeting. Moving before the altar, the *miko* does not represent—she manifests.

In ceremonies, the *miko* prepares offerings with delicate hands, positions elements precisely, sings hymns that calm and awaken. Her presence is discreet, but fundamental. She sustains the ritual's harmony with the silence of one serving the invisible. She does not explain. She reveals. The shrine, in her presence, becomes lighter, more attentive, more alive.

Many *miko* serve temporarily, during youth, before marriage. But there are those who, moved by deep vocation, remain. And there are also those who transcend the role of assistants and become full priestesses—a possibility that, though less common, has expanded in recent decades. Women today can be ordained priestesses, conduct rituals, recite *norito*, administer shrines. And when they do, they do not imitate male priesthood. They imprint their own vibration, their own spiritual cadence.

Women's role in Shinto was never secondary. Even in eras when patriarchy asserted itself in other religious traditions, Japanese shrines continued to shelter the feminine. Some of the most revered deities in the Shinto pantheon are female: Amaterasu, the sun goddess, origin of the imperial lineage; Konohanasakuya-hime, goddess of the cherry blossom and volcanoes; Ame-no-Uzume, the goddess of dance, joy, and revelation. Each carries a distinct force, but all reveal the vitality of the feminine as creative and ordering power.

Woman, exercising priesthood, does not just repeat rites—she channels this spiritual lineage. She aligns herself with these archetypal forces governing life, beauty, time, and transformation. Her presence in the shrine is more than a function—it is an affirmation that the sacred has no fixed gender, but manifests according to spirit and purity of intention.

In communities, the presence of women as spiritual figures is also welcomed naturally. At local festivals, it is often the older ladies who lead processions, keep ancient chants alive, teach children gestures and rites. They were not ordained by institutions, but by the very continuity of tradition. They are priestesses by experience, heritage, silent devotion.

Intuition, a quality often marginalized in rational contexts, is a legitimate form of spiritual knowledge in

Shinto. Woman, with her sensitivity to cycles, emotions, non-verbal language, finds in this field a deep affinity with the ways of the kami. The Shinto god does not impose—it insinuates. Does not speak loudly—it whispers. And hearing these whispers requires the fine listening that the feminine, in its fullest form, carries.

In purification rituals, female presence is often the element that softens and harmonizes the spiritual field. Offering sacred branches, leading liturgical song, sustaining silence with presence, the priestess creates space for the kami to manifest. There is no hierarchy between her and the male priest. There is complementarity. The balance between forces that, united, make the shrine a mirror of the natural order.

The rise of formal priestesses in modern Shinto represents not a rupture. It represents a return. A rebalancing. In a world trying to reorganize its forms of power, Shinto offers a subtle example of how feminine and masculine can coexist in the sacred without exclusion. And this coexistence arises not from decrees. It arises from practice. From mutual reverence. From the recognition that the kami responds to sincerity, not gender.

Woman, exercising priesthood, also brings the dimension of care. She observes details, notes alterations in the energetic field, perceives unspoken emotions of devotees. Her listening is broader. Her gaze, more symbolic. And by welcoming, guiding, calming, she fulfills the primary function of the sacred: leading back to harmony.

In some shrines, groups of women gather to keep rites alive. They sew vestments, clean paths, care for flowers, recite prayers. They do this without public recognition, without expectation of reward. They do because they know. And this knowing, transmitted from mother to daughter, grandmother to granddaughter, keeps alive an invisible flame sustaining tradition's continuity.

Woman, in Shinto priesthood, is not exception. She is root. And as root, she sustains, even if unseen. Her strength lies in constancy. In care. In beauty that seeks no spotlight. Her presence is what makes sacred space habitable, sensitive, fertile.

At the end of a ritual day, when candles are extinguished and silence settles again in the shrine, the priestess gathers objects with firm, gentle hands. She cleans the altar as if caressing a living being. She folds cloths respectfully. She remains. Because her service ends not with the rite—it continues in how she walks, speaks, lives. She is priestess not only when wearing ceremonial attire, but in every daily gesture. Because the sacred, for her, is a permanent state of attention.

In the recollection of daily gestures, female priesthood reveals its deepest nature: a spirituality that does not announce itself, but infiltrates the folds of time, space, and presence. Woman, when acting in the sacred, does not create ruptures—she reinforces bonds. Her practice is not just liturgical, but existential. With each silent offering, she reaffirms the idea that the spiritual is not separate from life, but its continuity in another, subtler tone. Her body, voice, listening become instruments of a liturgy extending beyond the altar, reaching the everyday as extension of the divine.

This way of being in the world transforms female priesthood into a living reference of balance and permanence. Woman seeks not to dominate the rite—she feels it. Claims not spaces by imposition, but by fidelity to a call preceding any system. Her spiritual knowing is intertwined with practice, care, silent transmission. And when she conducts a ritual or simply cares for sacred space, she imprints her energetic signature, the one making the environment more welcoming, more integral, more receptive to the kami's presence.

Thus, the feminine in Shinto is not accessory or concession—it is original pulsation of the sacred, founding force continuing to nourish the present with the wisdom of the invisible. In the end, the priestess remains not because someone placed her there, but because she never ceased to be. Her role predates institutions, is older than records, more resilient than structures. She is the silent guardian of the shrine's spirit, the flame not extinguished, the listening that welcomes, the gesture that heals. And therefore, even when no one else observes, when bells cease and offerings are collected, her presence continues filling the space like a sacred echo needing no voice to be heard.

# Chapter 13
# Sacred Dances

There is a language preceding words. A form of communication depending not on sound, nor writing, but vibrating in the body, air, and ancestral memory of peoples. This language is dance. In Shinto, it is not performing art, nor spectacle. It is rite. It is gesture that summons, awakens, attracts the presence of the gods. It is called *kagura*—the sacred dance.

The origin of *kagura* is intertwined with one of Shinto's most beautiful founding myths: the episode where Amaterasu, the sun goddess, hides in a cave after feeling offended and humiliated by her brother Susanoo. Darkness settles over the world. Cold, chaos, silence dominate the land. The gods, gathered, try in vain to convince her to emerge. Until one goddess, Ame-no-Uzume, decides to dance. She climbs onto a tub, tears her clothes, shakes her hips, lets out laughter. The gods, surprised, laugh. Laughter echoes. Curiosity awakens Amaterasu. She peeks at the cave entrance. And, seeing the reflection of her light in a mirror placed there, is seduced by her own beauty. She comes out. And with her, light returns to the world.

This narrative is not a static legend. It is a spiritual key. It shows that joy, movement, sensuality, art have power to heal, summon, restore order. Uzume's dance was not futile—it was necessary. And therefore, in her honor, and in honor of the light manifesting in the moving body, *kagura* was born.

Shinto sacred dances are not improvisations. Each step, each inclination, each turn has meaning. There is no rush. Beauty lies in precision. Arms move like branches in wind. Hands describe forms evoking nature's cycles. Feet touch ground respectfully, as if awakening the earth. The rhythm is not frantic. It is meditative. And the body becomes, itself, an altar.

There are two main types of *kagura*: *miko kagura*, danced by priestesses—*miko*—within shrines, and *sato kagura*, presented at festivals and community spaces. *Miko kagura* is more introspective, marked by delicate gestures, use of handbells (*suzu*), *sakaki* branches, and long sleeves floating like clouds. The dancer displays no exaggerated emotion. Remains restrained, serene, like a channel opening to the kami. Her presence is prayer in motion.

*Sato kagura*, conversely, is more popular and theatrical. Includes masks, drums, flutes, dramatic representations of myths. In it, dancers interpret episodes like Susanoo's battle with the eight-headed dragon, or the creation of islands by the couple Izanagi and Izanami. Dance becomes narrative. But even so, does not lose sacredness. Because even in enactment, the purpose is invocation. Attracting the gods. Opening space for their presence.

At festivals, *kagura* may be presented on raised stages within shrine grounds, called *kagura-den*. There, musicians play traditional instruments like *taiko* (drum), *hichiriki* (double-reed flute), and *shō* (mouth organ emitting ethereal chords). Music does not accompany—it conducts. Dictates gesture's timing, space's emotion. And dancers move in conformity with this sonic flow. No choreography to admire. A vibrational field to access.

The audience, meanwhile, does not watch in the Western sense. Participates with soul. Opens itself to what happens. Recognizes what unfolds before eyes is not spectacle, but bridge. Many, seeing the dance, feel tears for no apparent reason. Others, sudden warmth. Still others, state of deep tranquility. *Kagura* acts on the invisible. Acts on the soul.

In some ancient shrines, especially mountain regions, archaic forms of *kagura* preserved for centuries exist. In them, dancers wear masks of wood or clay, representing kami, animals, ancestors. Masks are not accessories. They are channels. Wearing them, the dancer ceases to be himself. Becomes vehicle. And in this state of "self-forgetting," allows kami to manifest. The borrowed body dances with the spirit inhabiting the air. Not rarely, these dances last hours, cross the night, end at dawn. And at the end, what remains is not exhaustion. Is a purified field. A community reunited. A people again in harmony with heaven and earth. *Kagura*, thus, is not entertainment. Is maintenance of cosmic order. Is spiritual service.

Those who dance *kagura* do so not out of vanity. No fame, nor glory. There is discipline. Devotion. Training is long. Begins in childhood, transmitted orally, with silent observation, patient repetition. Movements not learned from books. Learned by body. And body learns by listening. Each muscle educated to recognize right gesture, right timing, exact point where kami can enter.

*Kagura* also teaches art is not secondary. It is essential. In world valuing only reason, calculation, productivity, Shinto recalls body in state of beauty is portal. And dancing, when done truthfully, is praying with entire body. Sacred dance seeks not audience. Seeks presence. Presence of spirit. Presence of kami. Presence of dancer.

In many homes, simplified versions of *kagura* practiced on special dates. Mothers dance to thank for children's birth. Elder women dance to protect descendants. Men and women dance together around fire. Circle forms. And time transforms. Because in dance, time not linear. Spins. Returns to origin. Retraces light's path.

Reflecting on *kagura*, one understands Shinto is not faith of words. Faith of gestures. Postures. Bodies offered in reverence. And that is why dance occupies such high place: unites physical with ethereal. Unites muscle with myth. Unites sweat with sacred. Those who witnessed true *kagura* know something changes. Even without understanding, feel. Because there, between pulsating drum, floating veil, gaze lost on altar, there dwells the kami. And the space opened does not close soon. Remains. Continues dancing inside whoever saw it.

The sacred movement of *kagura* does not end with the ritual's conclusion—it lingers in the bodies and hearts of those who witnessed it. Like a bell's reverberation, its presence echoes within, adjusting internal frequencies, awakening forgotten layers of human sensitivity. The gesture that seemed simple reveals itself as a portal. The repetition of steps, a path of return. It is not a dance to be interpreted—it is a dance to be traversed. And, traversing it, the individual realigns with existence's primordial rhythm, the one pulsing even before language, resonating still today in shrines where time is spiral.

This dimension of dance as bridge between worlds reminds us the body is not mere instrument: it is territory of revelation. In *kagura*, the body becomes nature's mirror—now light as wind, now firm as mountain, now fluid as rivers. The dancer does not show off, offers themselves. And in this offering, participates in liturgy larger than themselves. When the kami is welcomed by pure gesture, dance not only represents sacred: makes it present.

Thus, the rite is not limited to the shrine. Spreads to the world. Each person touched by *kagura* carries vibrant memory of this passage, carries within the spark of sacred that danced before their eyes. And that is why *kagura* remains alive. Because depends not on audience, nor fame, nor written record. Depends only on available body, consecrated space, true intention. As long as someone dances with world's spirit, as long as feet touch ground as if kissing earth, the light Amaterasu brought back will never extinguish. It will continue being born, not just in sky, but in heart of each who understands dancing is, fundamentally, way of remembering who we are.

# Chapter 14
# Sounds and Symbols

There are places where nothing needs saying. Where the sound of a bell echoing in the wind suffices to quiet the spirit. Where the sight of a red arch before ancient trees is enough for the heart to recognize the border between the common world and the world of the kami. Shinto is a tradition where language is not limited to words. It extends to sounds, symbols, forms filling space and shaping atmosphere. The invisible speaks, and does so through beauty.

Sound has power. In Shinto, it serves not just to fill silence, but awaken it. The *suzu*, the small bell hung at shrine entrances, is not merely decorative. It calls the kami. Its vibration dispels impurities, breaks through layers of distraction, tunes the soul to sacred space. Arriving at a shrine, the visitor rings the bell before offering. As if saying: "I am here. Awake. Present." And the metallic sound spreading through air carries this presence.

The sound of clapping is also central. Clapping twice before the altar is more than tradition—it is ritual gesture. Claps mark the start of communication with gods. Cut through dispersion. Align body, mind, spirit. Awaken kami and practitioner. A dry, rhythmic sound reverberating not just in air, but soul. And in the interval between claps, silence settles. Silence not empty, but full. Full of listening.

There are also drums—*taiko*—announcing festivals, dances, processions. Their sound is deep, profound, bodily. The drum vibrates in earth, wood, body of player. Sound of birth, passage, invocation. Marks rhythm of community life and collective rite. When *taiko* plays, no one remains indifferent. Speaks to body before intellect. Invites participation.

Traditional ritual music—*gagaku*—combines instruments like *shō*, *hichiriki*, *koto*, creating soundscapes leading not to recognizable melodies, but states of mind. Music heard not just with ears, but entire body. Reorganizes inner space. Its long notes, pauses, rare timbres, all contribute to atmosphere where time dissolves and kami can approach.

But not only sound communicates. Visual symbols are silent portals. The *torii*, with its simple form of two vertical pillars linked by two horizontal beams, is Shinto's most iconic symbol. Protects not with barriers—delimits with presence. Crossing it, visitor enters another field of reality. Even if space beyond *torii* seems identical to space before, something changes. Body knows. Soul knows. The *torii* closes not, but opens. And its color, usually red or orange, not casual. Color of life, protection, sacredness. Color repelling evil, inviting attention.

Another recurring symbol: *shimenawa*, braided rice straw ropes, hung in sacred places—ancient trees, special stones, portals. Indicate kami resides there, or space is pure manifestation of sacred. Pendant white paper strips, called *shide*, flutter in wind like silent tongues. Speak not, but say. Explain not, but point.

Ritual attire also symbolic language. White of priests, *miko*, devotees in purification, not absence of color. Fullness. Purity. Fabric reflecting all light. Dressing in white declares oneself clean, available, receptive. Opens body to kami passage. Red of *miko* represents vitality, protection, fertility. Colors say what words cannot reach.

Then there are *ofuda*, paper or wood talismans consecrated in shrines. Contain kami name, placed at home, in *kamidana*, as extensions of sacred space. Not amulets in superstitious sense. Presences. Energy focuses. One maintaining them respectfully, cleaning, revering, cultivates not just protection, but connection.

*Omamori*, small fabric amulets with specific blessings—for health, studies, travel protection, fertility—are ways to keep kami close. Value not in object, but relationship represented. Devotee carries as reminder. Spiritual anchor. Sign of not walking alone.

There are also *ema*, small wooden plaques for writing wishes, thanks, vows. Hung on structures within shrines. Each carries voice of a heart. Request for healing. Thanks for victory. Hope facing unknown. Together, *ema* form silent chorus of humanity. And kami read. Read not with eyes, but presence.

*Tamagushi, sakaki* branches adorned with paper strips, offered in ceremonies as gesture of reverence. Green branch represents life. White paper, purity. Act of rotating branch, placing before altar is gestural poem.

Movement speaking: "I offer my best. With beauty. Order. Surrender."

Everything in Shinto is symbol. But not symbol as arbitrary representation. Symbol as epiphany. Revelation. World needs not explanation—needs honoring. And symbols are language of this honor. Translate not sacred—make accessible. Not external signs—inner paths. Therefore, one visiting shrine, even without knowing, without understanding, feels. Something changes. Something aligns. Because symbols speak directly to spirit. Transcend barriers of language, culture, belief. Are universal. Eternal. Alive.

Shinto teaches everything communicates. Bell's sound. Roof's curve. Bending bamboo. Moss-covered stone. Paper dancing in wind. Space between two *torii*. Way body walks approaching altar. All message. All presence. All kami.

And when devotee, in silence, lets self be touched by these sounds and symbols, enters field of deep listening. Learns read world with other eyes. Hear with heart. Perceive with soul. And in this state, each gesture becomes rite. Each space, sanctuary. Each instant, call.

Amidst this universe of sounds and symbols, the Shinto practitioner rediscovers sensitivity as a form of wisdom. Seeks understanding not just with mind, but whole body, open senses, awakened attention. Ritual isolates not from world—reintroduces with different listening. Vibration of *suzu*, beat of *taiko*, design of *shide* fluttering in wind: each element becomes invitation be more whole, present, true. Sacred space is not another world. Is this world, perceived delicately, reverently.

This sensitive presence allows devotee decipher shrines' full silence. Necessary not know all names, nor understand all gestures. What matters is willingness feel, let soul respond unhurriedly to symbols' call. When body bows, hands join, gaze rests respectfully on *torii*, practitioner participates language traversing time. And in this simple, yet full gesture, world re-enchants—not by something added, but what revealed. Symbol, after all, hides not: unveils.

That is why Shinto imposes not with dogmas, but reveals with gestures. Demands not blind faith, but clear attention. Sounds and symbols filling its rites testify spirituality needing no explanation to be lived. Conversely, less one tries translate, more understands. Because kami speaks in world's language, and world speaks to those willing listen. Bell, rope, paper, wood— all vibrate in unison with seeking spirit. And in this silent harmony, each sound, each symbol becomes passage. Becomes presence.

# Chapter 15
# Rites of Passage

Existence is not a straight line. It unfolds in cycles, curves, spirals repeating and renewing subtly. In Shinto, each stage of human life is accompanied by rites not merely marking time, but consecrating it. These moments, known as rites of passage, are not social formalities—they are spiritual transitions. Birth, childhood, youth, marriage, longevity: each milestone celebrated reverently, for each represents change of state, renewal of divine presence in individual and community.

The first of these rites is *hatsumiyamairi*, newborn's first shrine visit. Usually performed on thirty-first day of life for boys, thirty-third for girls, this ritual marks baby's formal introduction to spiritual world. Carried by parents, grandparents to local shrine, dressed traditionally, wrapped tenderly, expectantly. Priest performs brief ceremony before altar, offering prayers to kami, asking protection, health, harmonious growth. Child understands not with mind, but soul recognizes gesture. From this day, recognized by gods as part of human community. And life, still in early days, already intertwines with sacred's invisible thread. *Hatsumiyamairi* not just for baby—also rite for parents.

Marks start new phase, with responsibilities, joys, challenges. Trip to shrine way of declaring: "We are not alone. We are three now. And seek walk with gods." Shrine, in turn, welcomes new life gently. Demands nothing—only presence.

As years pass, child grows. Around ages three, five, seven, another fundamental rite performed: *Shichi-Go-San*, literally "seven-five-three." In this ceremony, children wear traditional attire—colorful kimonos, *hakama*, silk sashes—visit shrine thank for health received so far, ask blessings for next growth cycle. Boys taken to temple ages three, five; girls, three, seven. Moment of visible beauty, shared joy, but also deep spiritual significance. Childhood not seen as interval, but sacred part of path. And each year lived worthy celebration.

During *Shichi-Go-San*, children receive *chitose-ame*, long candies wrapped paper decorated images cranes, turtles—longevity symbols. Name means "thousand-year candy," expressing wish child's life be long, prosperous, happy. More than gift, offering in form sweetness. Sweetness desired for destiny.

Reaching youth, new rites mark individual's transition. Though Shinto lacks fixed ritual for majority, *seijin shiki* ceremony, held at age twenty, profoundly influenced by Japanese spiritual sensitivity. In it, youths recognized full members society, assume responsibilities, reaffirm commitment community. Many choose visit shrine this day, thank for childhood cycle, ask wisdom for new paths. Young women wear *furisode*—kimonos long, elaborate sleeves—young men wear suits or ceremonial *hakama*. Day marked by pride, beauty, introspection. Youth before altar, seeking not party, but direction.

Among all rites of passage, perhaps none more wrapped symbolism than *shinzen kekkon*, marriage before gods. Ceremony unites not just two individuals, but two lineages, histories, life paths. Couple, dressed formally—bride absolute white, groom dark *hakama*—led to shrine altar. There, before priest, family, rite performed. No extravagance. Order. Restrained beauty. Reverence.

During wedding, couple performs ritual *san-san-kudo*—three sips sake, repeated three times, totaling nine sips. Number three represents continuity, nine fullness. Each sip more than gesture: silent vow communion, sharing, presence. Sake symbol life, fermentation transforming simple into sacred. Drinking together, couple seals not just contract, but invisible promise. Kami witness. And ceremony's end, couple bows before altar as offering selves mutually before cosmos.

Later life, rites of passage cease not. Aging also celebrated. Sixtieth birthday, *kanreki* performed, marking return original zodiac cycle, symbolizing spiritual rebirth. Ages seventy, seventy-seven, eighty, eighty-eight, new celebrations held, known as *kiju*, *shichiju-shichi*, *beiju*, *hachi-ju-hachi*. Each not just time count. Recognition life extends, gods sustain, body may age, but spirit becomes ever more refined. In these longevity rites, family gathers. Children, grandchildren honor elders. Gratitude manifests gifts, prayers, words, food prepared attentively. Elder seen link between generations, living ancestral presence. Being honored, also transmits blessings. Not with speeches, but gaze. Silent wisdom who lived, remained clean-hearted.

Important note: though Shinto intensely celebrates life, death, conversely, treated discreetly. Carrying impurity energy, *kegare*, funeral rites traditionally associated Buddhism, dealing with afterlife, rebirth, suffering. Shinto, centering on present, here and now, purity, continuity, focuses celebrating what still pulses. Even so, dead not forgotten. Revered as ancestors, kami continuing influence living world. But mourning, funeral, contact lifeless body—domains treated modestly, kept away shrines preserve purity field.

Each rite of passage in Shinto, therefore, moment reintegration. Reintegration individual into existence's larger cycle. Reintegration community into spiritual axis. Reintegration life into kami flow. Nothing done by chance. Nothing gratuitous. Each gesture sewn carefully. Each word intoned intentionally. Each offering expression gratitude.

Living according Shinto learn perceive these milestones spiritual transition points. Not just birthdays or family ceremonies, but instants time opens. And when time opens, gods pass. Enter not thunderously— enter light wind. And if soul attentive, feels. Responds.

These rites of passage reveal that, in Shinto, life is celebrated in its entirety, as a path deserving attention at every step. Each cycle is treated not as repetition, but deepening—a more sensitive dive into the experience of existing. Time, in these moments, runs not: suspends.

And in this open interval between yesterday and tomorrow, the sacred now settles. The shrine, receiving newborn or elder, witnessing vow of love or youthful thanks, transforms into mirror of life in purest form. In it, human finds place be, just be, be fully.

These ceremonies, even simple, carry depth touching invisible. Gathering generations same gesture, rites build bridge between what was, is, will be. Restore sense belonging, continuity, connecting individual lineage, land, gods. And though marked formalities, attire, symbolic objects, true power lies in intention inhabiting them. In silent reverence, restrained step, sincere offering, rite fulfills role. Shinto teaches, thus, not just about passing through life, but marking presence in it—with respect, lightness, awareness. And perhaps this greatest teaching these rites: living is sacred. Not because life perfect, but because pulses, changes, insists. And each change, Shinto extends altar. Altar can be shrine, but also grandmother's lap, touch joined hands, silence preceding prayer. In these passages, no promises eternity—recognition ephemeral beauty instant. And that suffices. Because where true presence exists, kami approach. And where kami pass, life ignites.

# Chapter 16
# The Way of the Family

The home, in Shinto, is not just a space for coexistence. It is a sacred field where the kami make themselves present daily. The family, in its simplest or broadest configuration, is perceived as a spiritual cell—a microcosm where values of order, reverence, continuity are cultivated as silent offerings. This is not moral idealization. It is spiritual reality: where bonds lived respectfully, where memory ancestors exists, where gestures gratitude occur, there sacred establishes naturally.

Shinto imposes no family dogmas, legislates not fixed structures. Recognizes what is alive, relational, ancestral. Each family link between past, future, visible world, invisible worlds. Parents not just caregivers—transmitters spirit. Children not just individuals forming—extensions lineage, bearers sacred breath from ancestors. And grandparents, with silent presence, pillars sustaining time's verticality. Through them, memory dies not. Transforms into wisdom.

Ancestor worship one most intimate, constant practices everyday Shinto. Even if, many cases, performed also through Buddhist rites, spirit profoundly Shinto: honor who came before, recognize life begins not self, continues through self. Many homes, small altars—*kamidana, butsudan*—coexist, dedicated gods, ancestors. These spaces compete not. Complement. Kami, ancestor share same field presence. Both sources protection, inspiration, spiritual connection.

Ancestors not distant figures. Present family meals, commemorative dates, stories told grandchildren, photographs preserved carefully. Festivals like *Obon*, celebrate temporary return ancestral spirits earth. Families gather, clean tombs, light lanterns guide spirits, receive them food, music, reverence. No sadness. Reunion. Separation living, dead not definitive—only form. Spirit remains. Where remembered love, continues acting.

Family also place learn value *wa*—harmony. Harmony not absence conflict, but willingness respect natural order things. Elder imposes not—guides. Younger submits not—learns. Each role seen spiritual function, not authoritarian hierarchy. Mother, preparing meal attentively, offering more than nutrition—cultivating presence. Father, keeping space clean, safe, preserving field where kami dwells. Children, learning thank, greet, care objects, being initiated sacred path.

Family rituals need not formality be authentic. Joint visit shrine beginning year. Moment silence before altar before sleep. Practice greeting sun morning. Sharing food brief prayer. All acts devotion lived intimate community. Home becomes, thus, extension temple. Family life, continuous expression spirituality.

Children's education Shinto spirit not by imposition. Happens example. Seeing parents bow before altar, participating temple cleanings, wearing ceremonial kimono carefully, child internalizes values beyond words. Learns world inhabited presences. Respect not rule—way being. Gratitude not demand—natural response life's gift.

Even modern times, family structures diversify, Shinto continues offer spiritual field capable welcoming new forms coexistence. What matters not configuration, but quality relations. Where care, listening, respect exist, there kami remains. Family, more than legal or cultural concept, vibration. Where vibration resonates harmony, sacred manifests.

Marriage, for example, seen not just union two individuals, but two lineages. Shinto matrimonial rites recognize, uniting, couple also integrates ancestors, protector kami, histories. New family born not zero—continuation many cycles meeting. Therefore, establishing home, many couples set up *kamidana*, begin own devotional practices, care transmit children sense reverence, gratitude.

Child's birth, as seen *hatsumiyamairi* rites, reason great spiritual celebration. Entire family involved. Child's growth accompanied ceremonies marking not just time passage, but spirit's blossoming. Each year lived celebrated life's conquest, kami grace, continuity's victory.

Care elders also reflects this awareness. Not discarded, nor invisibilized. Honored living mirrors past. Stories, gestures, silent blessings—all sources learning, strength. Home where elder lives seen sacred space. When departs, presence dissolves not. Transforms family kami. Becomes invisible guardian lineage. Each time remembered, spirit strengthens. Lives.

Way of family, therefore, not just human course. Spiritual journey. Demands attention, presence, willingness care. Offers, return, deepest belonging sense one can experience. Knowing not alone. Part something larger. Invisible threads linking generations. Silent continuity sustaining each gesture.

Living Shinto family allow spirituality infiltrate most common moments: washing dishes, folding clothes, arranging house, sharing simple meal. Transform everyday liturgy. Home altar. Relation prayer. And this way living, gods not just distant entities. Become members house. Sit table. Observe tenderly. Protect firmly.

This spirituality permeating everyday family relies not grand revelations or extraordinary moments. Sprouts gesture repeated consciously, silent listening, mutual respect cultivated day after day. Shinto, recognizing sacred ordinary flow life, teaches divinity not distant, but immanent—hidden affection preparing meal, care welcoming sick relative, reverent silence before ancestral photograph. All done awakened heart becomes offering. All lived gratitude firms bonds between worlds.

Home, this sense, becomes space continuity not just biological, but spiritual. Value transmission not rules, but affective impregnation. Child observing adults revere elders, growing hearing stories charged respect, humor, participating small domestic celebrations enchantment, absorbs worldview where everything has soul, everything interconnected. Thus, home ceases just shelter, transforms field sensitivity formation, where reverence taught not—lived. And living thus, presence, simplicity, spirit communion, family becomes cosmos mirror. Cycles mirror nature's cycles; joys, sorrows reflect universe flows. Nothing lost remembered love. No gesture small born care. And this intertwining generations, visible, invisible, human, divine, manifests lineage true strength: not burden, but blessing. Not past, but continuity.

# Chapter 17
# Community Harmony

There exists a silent force sustaining cohesion among people, keeping neighbors united, communities alive, traditions preserved. This force arises not from laws or political structures. Springs from shared experience sacred. In Shinto, this force called community harmony, roots itself relationship between kami, people revering them. Each neighborhood, village, city, even amidst modernity, carries shrine its heart—dwells protector kami that collectivity, *ujigami*. *Ujigami* not generic god. Specific. Lives among people. Walks same streets, observes same fields, blesses same homes. Not just revered—part community.

This direct relation kami, social group differentiates Shinto many spiritual traditions. Here, divine distances not from world—inserts itself. And this insertion born deep sense belonging, feeling part something larger, alive, invisible.

Local shrine not just prayer space. Gravitational center community life. There seasonal rituals occur, weddings, birth blessings, harvest thanksgivings. There protection sought times epidemics, natural disasters, social crises. And there, too, celebrated joy encounters, group strength, tradition continuity. Constant presence shrine, its kami promotes stability. Speaks not, but guides. Imposes not, but sustains.

During *matsuri*, this link kami, community becomes visible, vibrant. Streets fill color, music, movement. Children, youth, adults, elders participate together. Each has function: carry *mikoshi*, prepare food, clean spaces, organize decorations, recite prayers, dance, sing. Festival produced not—lived. Expression collective body harmony spiritual. Kami, this moment, not just altar—carried streets, sees faces, hears voices. Community feels presence.

This shared experience sacred generates bonds depending not personal affinities. Different people, ages, professions, worldviews, become part same flow. Not imposition, but tradition. All know that kami belongs all. Suffices create solid base coexistence. Mutual respect grows, not fear punishment, but awareness divine presence observing all. Shame failing other born gratitude, not chastisement. And this healthy shame—sense collective responsibility—maintains social order.

Even large cities, frantic rhythm seems swallow silence, Shinto finds ways remain present. Small shrines between tall buildings, hidden *torii* busy streets, purification spaces industrial areas—all expressions spiritual resistance. Kami remain. Those remembering them, even amidst rush, cultivate link rescuing fragmentation. Simple act stopping before altar, bowing head, clapping twice, silencing moment, reintroduces individual collective body. Not alone. Belongs.

Villages, connection even more visible. Shrine center life. Important decisions discussed there. Crises brought altar. Earth cycles—planting, growth, harvest—rhythmed rites. Begin not work without blessing. Open not road without prayer. Inaugurate not bridge without purification. Kami not formality. Presence. And presence gives security, meaning, continuity.

Times natural catastrophes, earthquakes, tsunamis, many Japanese find shrine not just physical shelter, but spiritual axis. There mourn dead, thank survival, rise again silence. Kami, these hours, promises not magical solutions. But permanence offers solace. Is there. Saw. Remains. And with this, people also remain.

This community dimension Shinto surpasses religion. Molds way living. Schools, for example, celebrate foundational anniversaries rites local shrine. Companies organize ritual visits beginning fiscal year. Sports, cultural events, public inaugurations—all can have ceremonial dimension. Kami recognized part journey. Doing so, collectivity reinforces sense identity.

Shinto, promoting this community harmony, demands not uniformity. Respects diversity, invites coexistence. Local kami compete not. Dialogue. Each community worships own god, recognizes, respects neighbor's god. When necessary, unite inter-shrine festivals, sealing spiritual alliances reflecting politics, economy, culture. Faith isolated not—interconnected.

This model can inspire modern world, so marked fragmentation, competition, individualism. Shinto shows society can be cohesive not force, but reverence. People united not fear, but gratitude. Common space, recognized sacred, becomes territory peace.

Community harmony born not chance. Cultivated. Requires time, repetition, dedication. Youth need included. Elders, valued. Differences, respected. Kami observes all. Where sincere effort maintain *wa*—harmony—remains. Where selfishness, distances. But where collaboration, beauty, care other, smiles. Presence becomes blessing.

In Shinto, community not just sum individuals. Living body, spiritual entity, extension divine will. Preserving rites, spaces, symbols, values, body stays healthy. Breathes, dances, celebrates. Remakes itself each cycle. And this continuous flow, kami walks alongside, invisible, but present.

The true strength of community harmony lies in its ability to traverse time without losing meaning. It demands not everyone think alike, nor act same way, but asks mutual listening, willingness share space, time, care. Kami dwelling local shrine same transiting discreetly among houses, inspiring solidarity gesture, sustaining link between departed, those yet come. And just as ritual repeats ancients' steps new intentions, community also reinvents self without losing roots.

This continuous reinvention makes community harmony living practice. When child participates first time festival, carrying small offering or wearing ceremonial attire, not just playing or following protocol—being welcomed place's spirit. When elder invited tell stories before shrine, not just reminisces—strengthens collective soul. Each person, occupying role presence, respect, contributes invisible weaving sustaining common good. And this generous intertwining, kami finds abode.

That is why, even facing world changes, community harmony remains essential value. Opposes not modernity—balances it. Demands not return past—invites conscious continuity. Each village, city, metropolis where divine presence still recognized human gesture, Shinto flourishes silently, sustaining bridges between people, visible, invisible. And while hands willing care common, listen respectfully, celebrate gratefully exist, there kami will remain—not legend, but living reality.

# Chapter 18
# Virtues of the Heart

Shinto does not impose a codified morality. It presents no lists of sins, dictates no universal behaviors, threatens no eternal punishments. Instead, it offers the practitioner a subtler, more internal, truer path: cultivating the virtues of the heart. They are not norms. They are qualities. Learned not by external imposition, but developed through sensitivity, repetition of gestures, contact with the sacred. Shinto teaches living well is living with sincerity, purity, respect, righteousness—not out of fear, but affinity with the kami.

At the center of this ethic lies the concept of *makoto*, a word escaping exact translation. *Makoto* is sincerity, but also truth, purity of intention, essential honesty. It is the undisguised heart, action without calculation, word without mask. An act performed with *makoto* need not be perfect—needs be true. That is why, in Shinto rituals, form may vary, but sincerity indispensable. Gods impressed not mechanical gestures. Respond intention, silent feeling vibrating behind gesture. And this feeling connects human divine.

*Makoto* is active virtue. Not passivity, not naivety. Inner posture openness, clarity, presence. Acting according one's conscience, without betraying values uniting individual natural order. Person living *makoto* needs not justify actions. Presence transmits trust. Speech has weight. Silence has density. Life becomes, little by little, offering.

Alongside this fundamental sincerity, Shinto deeply values purity—not just physical sense, but above all spiritual. Purity, here, ability keep heart light, mind clear, body harmony environment. Why so much talk purification. *Misogi*, *harae*, baths, silent rites, all point this cleansing being. Not about warding off moral evil—removing what clouds, weighs down, blocks vital energy passage. Pure heart not one never errs—one allowing self renew. Purity, Shinto, cyclical. Lost, recovered. No guilt, no punishment. Consciousness. When someone perceives distanced lightness, seeks purification. Purifying, rediscovers center. Continuous process, silent, humble. There character forged.

Third virtue sustaining Shinto path respect—not formality, but recognition sacred value everything exists. Respecting other respects kami inhabiting them. Respecting nature recognizes each stone, tree, water drop divine presence. Respecting tradition honors those came before, transmitted rites, preserved symbols. Respecting self cares own body, word, spirit. Japan, respect manifests everyday gestures. Way object handed both hands. Way body bows before altar, elder, guest. Care public environment, others' silence, spaces' aesthetics. All born not civil code, but spiritual ethic. Respect imposed not. Cultivated like rare flower—patience, constancy, attention details.

Fourth virtue, inseparable previous, righteousness. Not inflexible righteousness, but firmness one aligning living universe rhythms. Righteous person one not bowing selfishness, not corrupted immediate desire, maintains direction even facing difficulties. Not rigid—rooted. Therefore, can be flexible without losing self. Shinto, righteousness silent. Needs not proclaimed. Reveals acts. Honesty working. Integrity caring family. Sobriety facing grief. Courage recognizing error. Righteous person lives not please others, but keep alive flame *magokoro*—true heart. And this heart deviates not, because not bound interests, but life's deep meaning.

These four virtues—*makoto*, purity, respect, righteousness—not unattainable ideals. Practices. Daily paths. Ways approach kami, not complex rituals, but quality presence. Who cultivates them, even wordlessly, even silently, transforms world around.

Children's education, these virtues transmitted early. Not imposition, but example. Child seeing parents revere gods, participating cleaning rituals, taught thank before meal, learns young life gift. Living beautifully way repay gift.

Japanese society, shaped centuries Shinto influence, still preserves many traces these virtues. Sense order public spaces. Shared responsibility communities. Value aesthetics. Delicacy interactions. All expressions everyday spirituality. Even if many declare not religious, live Shinto spirit gestures.

World words many, actions few, Shinto offers different path. Demands not believe—demands live attention. Promises not paradises—offers harmony. Defines not sin—points inner disharmony. Doing so, invites human look within. Listen own breath. Align nature cycles. Recognize divine vibrating everything.

Shame, this context, not punishment. Compass. When someone acts against heart virtues, feels shame—not judged, but knows deviated harmony. Shame discreet, effective. Guides. Corrects. Therefore, Shinto ethical system both light, profound. Binds not—liberates.

Modern world, so marked external demands, moral conflicts, polarizations, can find solace Shinto. Not ready answer, but invitation. Invitation slow down. Silence. Pay attention. Live more truly, lightly, reverently. Because, end, what gods desire not perfection. Sincerity. And sincerity begins cultivating heart virtues. Simple, real, what pulses inside each being.

Living with the virtues of the heart is, therefore, an exercise in presence. Not about adhering to doctrine, but developing finer listening own feeling, world's subtle rhythm. Practitioner walking attentive this call begins perceive each moment offers opportunity express sincerity, purity, respect, righteousness. From how greets someone to how deals error committed, everything becomes chance attune invisible. This path, error not failure, but occasion return. Virtue not medal, but way being world.

This silent, natural dimension Shinto ethics reveals strength precisely absence imposition. Instead creating walls between right, wrong, invites subtlety perception, delicacy gesture, integrity built everyday. Heart cultivating *makoto* needs no applause. Soul seeking purity boasts not. Respect, righteousness, when true, flourish even anonymity. Perhaps this greatest beauty Shinto path: transforms ordinary sublime, not feats, but silent quality being. Thus, step by step, gesture gesture, life becomes offering. Home, work, casual encounters, solitude instants become stage inner flowering. And this flowering without rush, ambition, vanity, human approaches most essential: true heart, pulsing harmony all living. This state, no longer separation human, divine—only presence. Where sincere presence exists, there also kami.

# Chapter 19
# Education and Character

In Shinto tradition, educating means not just transmitting knowledge. Means shaping spirit, aligning behavior sacred rhythm, forming humans living harmony visible, invisible worlds. Shinto offers not formal pedagogical system, but inspires, own essence, form education based example, repetition significant gestures, respect nature, shared discipline, cultivation silent virtues. Education proclaiming not spiritual, but springs soil impregnated divine presence.

Japanese child, early years, learns space lives needs care. Hears not moral lesson—sees adults practicing. Learns beauty matters, cleaning not others' function, but everyone's duty, thanking more important demanding. Schools, spirit becomes concrete practice. Classroom organized students themselves. Bathrooms, hallways, stairs, all cleaned children's hands, daily. Act cleaning not punishment—learning. Daily rite humility, responsibility. No spectacular rewards. No humiliating punishments. What exists coexistence, example, environment valuing collective above selfishness. Group matters. Each one's presence affects all. Silence, respectful greeting, care materials, all teach, without saying, world needs care. Caring world begins self care.

Teacher, this context, not authoritarian figure. Extension values school aims cultivate. Positions self firmly, without imposition. Corrects presence. Above all, acts example. Teachers also clean, revere school space, transmit, through conduct, spirit wished awaken students. Authority born coherence. Education, thus, ceases just instruction become character transmission.

School ceremonies reflect this ethos. Beginning school year, common visit local shrine. School, teachers, staff, students, presents self before region's protector kami. Not religious obligation. Way recognizing wisdom gift, learning process sacred, each child's journey needs blessings. Ritual brief, simple, silent. Returning school, environment already impregnated sense reverence.

Even most playful activities, sports, cultural festivals, school fairs, marked spirit attention. Spaces decorated meticulously. Events prepared weeks advance. Improvise not casually. Each detail matters. Because everything expression. When learns care details, learns care own life. Aesthetic sense, here, not vanity. Spirituality. Search balance, lightness, natural beauty.

Absence dogmatic morality also striking characteristic. Shinto demands not student learn religious concepts, nor memorize mythological stories obligation. Conversely, values silence, listening, observation. Gods' stories told expressions human nature, metaphors harmony, conflict, reconciliation. Not absolute truths. Symbolic maps soul. Child, hearing Amaterasu, Susanoo, Uzume, recognizes self emotions, fears, impulses. Little by little, internalizes sense order these narratives reveal.

Discipline Japanese schools not rigid military sense. Rhythmic. Structures time, organizes body, guides mind. Daily routine, fixed schedules, silence moments, pauses food, cleaning, creates field inner stability. Stability essential character flourishing. Student learns not mercy impulses. Can restrain self. Choose. Collaborate. Process, also learns respect others' space.

Care school environment another direct extension Shinto spirit. Each object valued. Each material its place. Desks organized. Shoes changed entering school. Uniforms worn sobriety. No ostentation. Presence. Awareness space learns needs clean, ordered, harmonious. External order echoes student's interior. Feels part something larger. Understands, wordlessly, school not just building. Sacred field formation.

Cultivating this type environment, school needs not severe punishments, nor psychological control mechanisms. Student self develops healthy shame facing failure. Disrespects other, destroys what not belong, acts selfishly, feels dissonance. Not because someone punished, but because deviated harmony. Perception, born within, more transformative any imposed discipline.

Spiritual formation Shinto, therefore, happens not closed temples, nor formal classes. Happens everyday. Way student stands seeing teacher. Way listens classmates. Way bows entering environment. Patience preparing school food. Gratitude expressed before eating. All rite. All learning.

Character, here, forged like bamboo: flexible, strong, silent. Child needs not molded rigid rules. Needs field presence values grow tree. Field prepared attention, repetition, example. No rush. Time educates. Time, Shinto, cyclical, alive, sacred.

Results silent education manifest adult life. Respect professionals act. Order public spaces treated. Sense cooperation permeating team work. Care other, even disagreeing. Not perfect society. Society learned, implicit spirituality, living well begins how walks, speaks, treats space occupies.

This education model, process learning reduces not content, expands towards formation present, sensitive, integral spirit. Classroom becomes home extension, teacher kami reflection, school everyday succession small rituals sedimenting values without needing name them. When child learns put on shoes attention, fold cleaning cloth zeal, serve food gratitude, not just repeating gestures—internalizing posture towards life. Posture, even without theoretical explanation, silently molds character, water sculpting stone.

Education inspired Shinto reveals building good human requires not rigidity, but constancy. Coherence word, action, delicacy details, respect others' time, own space, all seeds sown fertile soil childhood. Seeds germinate not genius explosions, but discreet beauty daily discipline. Environment, rites, relationships—all educate. Thus, character formation ceases specialist task becomes shared task, lived all participating school community. Fertile field visible, invisible intertwine, child grows part larger whole, learning living respect, simplicity, attention is, itself, form wisdom. Character, understood here, reduces not morality or external behavior, pulses inner vibration aligned universal harmony. Educate, therefore, reveal vibration, allow express naturally. Process, each gesture, however simple, becomes link child, sacred inhabiting world.

# Chapter 20
# Work as Offering

In Shinto, there is no separation between sacred and everyday. Temple not only place kami manifests. Prayer not only gesture capable touching invisible. Offering, when sincere, can assume any form—true word, care gesture, silence moment, action done full dedication. This spirit work, activity often treated mere obligation or subsistence means, re-signified spiritual act. Working well serves gods. Executing task attention, purity intention, discipline, beauty, is, itself, form reverence.

Worker, Shinto universe, not production instrument—agent balance. Office, whatever it is, participates great cosmic order. Cook, preparing food, not just nourishes bodies—perpetuates vital energy kami offer earth. Farmer, caring rice paddy, not just harvests—honors seasons cycle, earth spirit, sun, rain gift. Artisan, molding wood, clay, paper, not just creates objects—channels beauty springing invisible world. Businessman, teacher, fisherman, engineer, all essentially offerers. Altar, this case, space action.

This perception radically transforms relation office. Work ceases burden. Becomes path. Path spiritual realization, values expression, community integration. Waking morning, one working *magokoro*—true heart—already begins day state worship. Cleans work environment prepares sanctuary. Organizes instruments positions altar elements. Receives colleague welcomes sacred guest. Performs tasks same zeal dedicate rite.

Many Japanese companies, still today, preserve practices directly linked Shinto spirit. Beginning fiscal year rituals performed local shrines, company representatives thank previous cycle, ask protection new one. Purification rites conducted before inaugurating new headquarters, factories, projects. Priest attends, recites prayers, offers *tamagushi*, consecrates space. Not superstition. Recognition: kami inhabits time, space, work, being part, needs harmonized.

Even small businesses usually maintain *kamidana* discreet point place. Daily, offer water, rice, sake. Light incense. Bow before altar. Follow chores. Offering precedes sale. Spirit precedes profit. Connection gods comes before result. Because working consonance natural flow, fruits arise without excessive effort. Sprout consequence, not obsession.

Shinto demonizes not prosperity. Perceives blessing, not isolated conquest. Profit, when fruit honest actions, becomes sign harmony. Harmony expresses also how success managed: gratitude, modesty, sharing. Company prospering makes larger offerings, supports festivals, sponsors community activities, invests preserving local shrines. Cycle closes. What received returned. What conquered blessed. Work, thus, ceases just economy—becomes spirituality action.

Shinto work ethic values continuous effort, humility facing process, pursuit excellence. Called *kodawari*, zeal perfection, clear expression this posture. Work not just deliver final product, but do well each stage. Food preparation, piece fitting, report writing, all done attention detail. Because each detail carries spirit executor. Spirit, aligned *magokoro*, transforms ordinary extraordinary.

Posture also manifests respect colleagues, silent cooperation gestures, environments organization. Common, end workday, all participate space cleaning. Workplace cared extension home, temple. No one destined collect others' trash—all collaborate. Daily gesture reaffirms space sacred, collective presence matters, harmony built small, constant actions.

Tiredness, when arises, not reason lament—sign vital energy donated. Therefore, rest also respected. Pauses made presence. Food consumed gratitude. Silence moments valued. Even spaces brief prayers, incense lighting, contact open sky. Work devours not time. Organizes time. Structures day. Therefore, imprisons not—liberates.

Perspective applied any culture, office, person. Just change gaze. Work needs not seen burden, punishment, system demand. Can be experienced gifts expression, opportunity serve collective good, inner development channel. Profession, then, transforms vocation. Routine, ritual.

Even simplest functions, spirituality flourish. Attendant smiling sincerely, driver driving carefully, cleaner cleaning attention, caregiver listening patiently—all, acting *makoto*, become offerers. Actions, even invisible society eyes, noted kami. Kami, silent attention, bless.

Japan, temples dedicated specific offices. Kami protecting fishermen, farmers, scholars, merchants. Each profession accompanied divinities understanding difficulties, joys. Seeking inspiration, protection, worker recognizes not alone. Effort participates something larger. Sweat, offered truth, also prayer.

Modern world, marked rush, competition, exhaustion, can rediscover balance recovering this spiritual sense work. Not romanticize toil, but return dignity. Remember body works temple. Time donated valuable. Energy invested builds not just products, services, but also bonds, memories, legacies. Shinto invites this reconnection. Look own office mission. Transform workspace altar. Wake gratitude. Begin day reverence. End journey silence. Because each action, when done attention, respect, beauty, becomes channel divine. This state consciousness, human works not just live—lives offer. Lives serve. Lives harmonize visible invisible.

This way living work requires not extraordinary occupations, nor prestigious titles. Asks presence. Gardener removing leaves attention, technician reviewing circuits precision, accountant organizing numbers clarity—all participate same principle: offer best self, even most discreet tasks, way honor life. Spirit transforms doing communion, everyday silent rite. When gesture integral, reverberates beyond action.

Purifies environment, strengthens character, elevates spirit. World around, even unnoticed, benefits vibration.

Working consciously, therefore, aligns greater flow organizing universe. Shinto shows no task small executed respectfully. Repetition not monotony—meditation. Effort not punishment—offering. Even errors, recognized humility, become part path. Each stumble reveals point purified. Each success firms link visible, invisible. Worker, thus, ceases just production agent: becomes conscious link earth, sky, concrete world, spiritual world. Bridge. Channel. Offering. Living this way, wholeness, zeal, true heart, human rediscovers dignity not what possesses, but what delivers. Work ceases reward waiting becomes expression own essence. This state, not position conferring value person, but purity living function. And thus, even amidst modern world noise, new quietude flourishes: born coherence, simplicity, devotion contained doing. Because where sincere effort exists, there also dwells kami—silent, invisible, but present each well-done gesture.

# Chapter 21
# The Way of Prosperity

In the heart of Shinto, prosperity is not treated as a distant ideal or a good reserved for a favored few. It is perceived as the natural consequence of living in tune with nature's rhythms, earth's cycles, and the invisible flow of blessings from the kami. When existence aligns with what is true, beautiful, and harmonious, abundance manifests. Not as a prize, but as an extension of an inner state. On the Way of the Kami, to prosper is to flourish—and this flourishing is accessible to all who live with gratitude, respect, and integrity.

Prosperity, for Shinto, takes multiple forms. It is not limited to money or material goods. It includes vibrant health, harmonious relationships, time well lived, inner tranquility, ancestral protection, connection with the land, the gods, and the community. True wealth is that which strengthens the spirit, deepens bonds, expands the capacity to serve. That is why, in shrines, requests for success are rarely unaccompanied by gestures of reverence and gratitude. The devotee does not demand—they offer. And in this sincere offering, the energy of abundance begins to circulate.

The kami associated with prosperity are numerous and close. Among them, Inari Ōkami stands out, deity of harvests, rice, fertility, business, and productivity. Inari is not an abstract god. He manifests in millions of small and large shrines scattered throughout Japan, recognizable by their rows of red *torii* and statues of foxes—his spiritual messengers. Merchants, farmers, entrepreneurs, and entire families visit his temples to ask for success in their endeavors, good harvests, protection against losses, fluidity in business. But before asking, they offer: rice, sake, money, *sakaki* branches, prayers. The act of offering is already a sign of understanding the silent pact between human and kami: give to receive. Share to grow.

Another path to prosperity in Shinto is the veneration of the Shichifukujin, the Seven Gods of Luck. Although this tradition incorporates elements of Buddhism and Chinese folklore, it became deeply rooted in Japanese culture and harmonized with the Shinto spirit. Each of these seven kami represents a dimension of good fortune: longevity, happiness, wealth, wisdom, courage, popularity, and fertility. They travel together on a boat called Takarabune, laden with symbolic treasures, arriving in homes at the turn of the year, bringing blessings for the new cycle. Images of these gods are distributed, drawn, venerated. They do not promise miracles—they remind people that prosperity results from communion with the good, the beautiful, the just.

Practices to attract and maintain prosperity are simple, yet charged with meaning. One is the making and use of *omamori*, amulets of protection and luck consecrated in shrines. There are specific *omamori* for business, exams, contracts, travel, investments. These small objects, usually made of fabric, contain within them a prayer, a kami name, a request. The devotee carries them respectfully, without opening or violating their integrity, knowing an invisible protective force resides there. They are not magical—they are reminders of the gods' presence and the need to act consciously.

Another symbolic instrument of prosperity is the *ema*, the small wooden plaque where devotees write their wishes. In shrines, thousands of these plaques accumulate before altars, forming a silent chorus of human aspirations: health, love, employment, overcoming challenges, growth, recognition. Each request is made humbly. Writing becomes a ritual gesture. And the kami, though silent, welcomes the wish. Promises not to fulfill it—promises to hear it. And in this hearing, there is already blessing.

There are also specific rituals for businesses. When opening a store, company, or new venture, many Japanese perform purification and consecration ceremonies. A priest is invited, the space symbolically cleansed with branches, bells, water, sacred words. The environment becomes fertile ground for success. And those working there begin to act with more responsibility, care, devotion. The space ceases to be merely commercial. Becomes extension of the temple. And work, as already seen, transforms into continuous offering.

At festivals, prosperity is also celebrated. During Tōka Ebisu, for example, merchants thank Ebisu, one of the seven gods of luck, for a year of good business.

They receive bamboo branches decorated with coins, small boats, fish, other symbols of abundance. These branches are taken home or to the shop, remaining throughout the year. They are not superstitious amulets—they are constant reminders that prosperity is gift and responsibility. And at cycle's end, returned to temple, burned in collective rite, replaced by new ones, symbolizing renewal.

Important to understand that, in Shinto, prosperity is never isolated. Always relational. One wishes not wealth just for self—wishes it benefit family, community, surroundings. Fortune excluding seen as imbalance. Abundance accumulating without sharing attracts isolation, loss meaning. Therefore, worship luck kami always tied values like gratitude, cooperation, reverence. Receiving good. Sharing better. This spirit keeps energy flowing.

Constant practice gratitude one most powerful ways maintain prosperity. Thank not just when something achieved. Thank always: morning, another day; before meals, food; end workday, effort completed; end cycle, lessons received. Gratitude aligns spirit. Aligned spirit natural magnet blessings.

Homes, abundance spirituality also manifests. *Kamidana*, domestic altar, becomes space thank gains, offer work fruits, ask guidance. Many Japanese families maintain custom placing part first rice harvested or bought before altar, symbolizing what nourishes body also nourishes relation gods. Nothing possessed alone. Everything given. What given, must be cared for.

Times crisis, Shinto offers serenity. Teaches cycles change, scarcity can be part path, important keep heart pure. Prosperity not absence challenges—ability remain integral facing them. Faith return balance sustains devotee difficult moments. Kami abandon not. Observe. Wait heart rediscover center.

Way Prosperity, then, inner journey before external. Way living, thinking, acting. Not magical rituals attract fortune, but existential posture based harmony. When human lives respectfully, works dedicatedly, shares generously, celebrates joyfully, thanks sincerely, becomes channel abundance. Where he is, life flourishes.

The flourishing of life, in this context, is not just a consequence of ethical conduct, but an expression of a living bond between the human and the sacred. This bond is built in the everyday—in the care for details, the intention permeating each action, the delicacy of a gesture. To prosper, then, is also to remain sensitive to the subtle manifestations of the divine: the scent of incense rising to the heavens, the breeze swaying the *sakaki* branches, the sound of prayers shared in unison. All this constitutes the living landscape where abundance becomes possible. Because, when one lives with reverence, reality transforms—and the common reveals its sacredness.

It is in this fertile field, built by attitudes of respect and communion, that the fruits of prosperity become lasting. There is no room for haste, empty accumulation, or obsession with performance. The Way of the Kami teaches that what comes quickly, goes quickly; that what is true matures over time, like rice in the fields. The prosperous life is one that respects timings, honors processes, embraces both winters and springs. Shinto spirituality points, thus, to a wealth that does not deplete—but renews continually, the more it is shared.

Thus, following the Way of Prosperity is accepting the invitation to live fully, not by goals to be achieved, but by states to be cultivated. The devotee seeks not to guarantee their future with promises or divine contracts, but walks side-by-side with the gods, with trust and openness. They know that as long as gratitude is in their heart, reverence in their acts, and generosity on their journey, abundance will accompany them—like shadow follows body in sun.

# Chapter 22
# Circle of the Seasons

Time, in Shinto, is not a straight line. It is cycle. Living spiral renewing each season, moon, birth, death. Time advances not—spins. This eternal turning, human finds chance reconnect, purify, restart. Seasons not just climatic divisions—expressions kami, rhythmic manifestations divine presence earth. Who learns read nature signs, learns live harmony what invisible eyes, palpable heart.

Japan, where Shinto flourished, seasons intense, distinct, clear signs. Spring brings ephemeral cherry blossom perfume. Summer carries vibrant weight expanding life. Autumn paints leaves red, gold, silence. Winter covers earth white, recollection. Each cycle, unique beauty, offers deep spiritual lessons. Shinto rites accompany rhythm, not just tradition, but know: kami speaks earth, who listens earth, listens kami.

Spring, awakening celebrated. Life returns softly, forcefully. Cherry blossoms bloom few days—this brief instant reveals impermanence teaching. Beauty not what lasts, but intensely lived. Festivals like Haru Matsuri fill shrines colors, laughter. Families, friends gather under blooming trees, not just celebrate nature, but celebrate renewal miracle. Sakura blossoming gods' greeting.

Visible blessing. Sitting its shadow, devotee contemplates not just tree—contemplates own soul flowering.

Summer brings heat, intensity. Fields fill life. Work arduous, but spirit expands. *Matsuri* take streets. Kami carried processions. Drums resonate collective heartbeat. Dances, offerings, floating lanterns river—all movement, invocation. Summer heat, human rediscovers vital force. Rites celebrate potency. Sweat becomes offering. Music, prayer. Night lit lanterns not just party—communion.

Autumn, rhythm slows. Leaves fall reminder everything returns earth. Harvest done. Grains gathered gratitude. Time thank, recollect little, look within. Autumnal festivals, rites new rice offering, silent depth. Offerings made not request—gratitude. Body calms. Heart quiets. Spirit prepares recollection. Leaves' red, kami paints farewell. Not end—transformation.

Winter, silence, time purification. Landscape turns white. Sounds muffled. Steps slow. Devotee enters state listening. Beginning year rituals, *Hatsumōde*, invite renewal. Shrines fill prayers new cycle. Even under snow, *torii* remains firm, sign sacred never absent. Cold not punishment—invitation interiority. Who allows self silence, hears more. Feels more. Becomes fertile soil what come.

But time, Shinto, limited not seasons. Marked also moon, agricultural cycles, life rites. Japanese ritual calendar intertwines solar, lunar fluidly. Each date bridge everyday, sacred. Festivals fixed not just calendar—fixed earth rhythm. Celebrate planting, sprouting, growing, harvesting. Doing so, people reaffirm connection life.

Shinto practitioner learns look sky, field reads sacred text. Passing cloud, changing wind, blooming flower, returning bird—all language. All sign. Soul, attuned rhythm, knows what do. Knows when act, withdraw, offer, thank. Life ceases struggle against time—becomes dance with it.

Harmony natural cycles not just poetic. Source health, emotional balance, practical wisdom. Who lives discord seasons, sickens. Who ignores earth signs, gets lost. Shinto teaches respecting cycles respects own essence. Human body made water, wind, earth. Everything affecting nature, affects also spirit. Therefore, purification rites not just symbolic—real. Help undo accumulation no longer necessary. Clean invisible dust soul.

Each season also invites virtue. Spring teaches lightness. Summer, courage. Autumn, gratitude. Winter, wisdom. Who observes nature, learns effortlessly. Who lives consonance it, walks gods. *Torii*, bell, altar, all important. But wind, flower, cold, heat also living altars. Devotee knows: where life, kami.

This cyclical time awareness helps dissolve anxiety. No rush where rhythm. No despair where renewal. Error committed purified. Cycle ending gives way another. What seems loss preparation new. Confidence existence flow one greatest offerings make gods. Confidence allows human live beautifully, even facing impermanence.

Shinto, living being relation. Other. Nature. Ancestors. Gods. All bonds woven time. Time not enemy—ally. Takes not away—transforms. Who understands, transforms together. Serenity. Reverence. Awakened spirit.

Living within this rhythm allows own heart beat earth compass, drum echoing heavens music. Each season, more than scenery, silent master inviting human observe self, review self, recreate self. Flower bloom or leaf fall, always subtle call consciousness: nothing permanent, but everything precious. Eternity not what remains same, but transforms grace. Thus, time ceases burden becomes melody—song leading soul back essential.

This wisdom cycles requires not erudition, just presence. Simple act picking fruit its time, silencing facing cold, thanking rain or harvest, becomes spiritual practice. Nature teaches wordlessly, Shinto invites listen whole body. Recognizing self part pulsating whole, human finds place—not earth dominator, but sensitive link visible, invisible. Belonging heals. Heals excess, rush, disconnection. Teaches walk slower, more whole, truer.

Following Circle Seasons, therefore, accept time's sacred dance humility, joy. Recognize moment everything, each moment carries own blessing. Fluid compass, devotee sheds rigidity welcomes impermanence expression life's own beauty. Then, living becomes offering. Being present becomes prayer. Time, previously feared passage, reveals path return most intimate, divine.

# Chapter 23
# Shrines Abroad

The kami know no borders. They are not bound to territory, nor limited by nationality or language. Wherever respect, purity, gratitude, sincerity exist, there their spirit can manifest. That is why, even outside Japan, Shinto remains alive. In distant communities, diverse continents, cities perhaps never seen cherry blossom, shrines emerge—discreet, silent, but charged same ancestral force pulsing *jinja* Japan. Worship kami crossed oceans, crossed time, today flourishes where least expected.

Shinto expansion beyond Japan not missionary project, nor conversion strategy. Happened because people. Because immigrants who, leaving lands, carried values, rites, amulets, gods. Arriving Brazil, United States, Peru, Argentina, Hawaii, Canada, many other places, people found new lands, cultures, but abandoned not spiritual roots. Where settled, created space sacred.

Brazil, for example, presence Shinto shrines dates first half 20th century, especially regions large concentration Japanese immigrants, São Paulo, Paraná, country interior. Best known Jinja Kaikan, located São Paulo south zone, houses Brazil-Japan Shinto Temple, consecrated 2015 presence priests come directly Japan.

There, rites conducted same precision, reverence observed Japanese temples. Space *misogi*, prayers, *sakaki* offering, purification rites, living presence kami Brazilian soil.

Each these spaces, something remains unchanged: *torii*. Red or orange structure, erected even amidst modern buildings or tropical fields, continues marking threshold profane world, sacred. Passing through same symbolic gesture, Tokyo or São Paulo, foot Mount Fuji or banks Tietê River. Devotee bows, claps, reveres, world changes. Matters not where body—spirit returns axis.

Shrines outside Japan follow same ritual calendar. Perform *Hatsumōde*, first year visit; organize *Shichi-Go-San*, rites children; celebrate *matsuri* traditional dances, music, food. Even unavoidable cultural adaptations, rites spirit preserved. Because essential not form, but sincerity. Sincerity depends not geography. Universal.

Priests trained Japan, officially recognized Shinto institutions, served various countries. Some direct descendants immigrants. Others foreigners who, deep devotion, dedicated study, practice, serve. Became bridges between cultures. Became channels continuity tradition which, though deeply rooted Japanese soil, has vocation world. Because kami speak human heart, heart has no nationality.

United States, shrines places like Hawaii, California. Peru, tradition flourished Nipo-Peruvian communities, many maintaining devotional practices home or community centers. Canada, Argentina, Mexico, families maintain *kamidana*, make daily prayers, celebrate local festivals adapted Shinto calendar. Flame remains lit. Kami, sensitive reverence, remains present.

What observed these contexts Shinto ability adapt without corruption. Accommodates new soil, maintains essence. Welcomes new practitioners without demanding renunciation other beliefs. Recognizes spirituality experience, not affiliation. Why non-Japanese descendants found this path source meaning, silent practice connection divine, way inhabit world more lightness, attention.

Shinto, lived outside Japan, challenges rigid notions religion. Imposes not baptisms, demands not oaths, prohibits not other paths. Merely invites. Invites purity. Invites silence. Invites respect nature, life, cycles. Who responds invitation, Tokyo, Buenos Aires, London, Nairobi, becomes part same flow.

Difficulties exist. Cultural distance, scarcity priests, general ignorance Shinto, religious prejudice. Obstacles prevent not kami manifesting. Where sincerity, remain. Where care space, time, other, descend. Where clean heart, awakened presence, dance. Even no *torii*. Even no altar. Even offering gesture, word, silence.

Nature, being kami main abode, present all planet corners. Mount Fuji not Brazil, but mountains house same silence. Okinawa sea bathes not Peru, but Pacific waves whisper same messages. Japanese forest grows not Canada, but pine, oak woods hide same whispers. Who walks landscapes spirit reverence, walks kami.

Shrine abroad not just physical construction. Symbol continuity. Body living tradition. Mirror people commitment soul. More still: bridge between worlds. Between Japan, country where stands. Between ancestral culture, multicultural present. Between visible, invisible. Between human, divine.

This bridge built not just wood, stone, rice paper—made daily gestures, shared memories, respectful silence before altar improvised shelf, garden, room corner. Shinto spirituality flourishes wherever care invisible, each shrine abroad, however small, extension Japanese spirit living not just aesthetics, but ethics reverence. Bell sound echoing São Paulo or Vancouver replicates not Japan—reveals sacred common language, understood all approaching open heart.

These transnational spaces, Shinto assumes even broader function: becomes bridge reconciliation land lives, whatever it is. Rites connect ancestral spirituality local winds, waters, forests, creating symbolic roots respecting new soil without forgetting old. Spirituality encounter. No demand ethnic belonging, nor exclusivity. Yes, invitation listen. Call presence. This coexistence, hybrid practices emerge, creative, profound, enriching both local culture, ancestors tradition.

Thus, shrines outside Japan not vestiges lost identity, but living signs spirituality renewing steps those continuing walk. Places time slows, gesture becomes prayer, distance turns proximity. Each one— even most modest, most isolated—carries kami silent promise: where respect, there also we be. Where beauty, there flourish. Where gratitude, there make ourselves present.

# Chapter 24
# Silent Conversion

In Shinto, no door closes, no ritual imposes. One approaching kami needs declare nothing, abandon nothing, prove nothing. Just live reverently. Just cultivate purity, gratitude, respect life, invisible. Thus, without announcements, formal initiations, promises, obligations, practitioner heart aligns gods rhythm. Conversion, this path, not rupture—silence. Not oath—practice. Not identity—attunement.

Unlike institutional religions structured around dogmas, codes, affiliations, creeds, Shinto requires no exclusivity. Denies not other beliefs, combats not other traditions, demands not renunciation. Not religion belonging, but presence. Person can be Christian, Buddhist, Muslim, atheist—still find Shinto way live more meaning. Because what offers not closed truth. Way being world lightness, sensitivity, harmony.

This openness makes Shinto discreet spirituality. Seeks not faithful. Welcomes walkers. Those approaching do so because something calls: shrine silence, hand clapping gesture, bell sound, *torii* beauty, offering simplicity. Reproducing gestures sincerely, already living path. Conversion not act—process.

Process begins instant person perceives kami everything, decides live up perception.

Interested wishing approach Shinto begins practice. No mandatory books, nor doctrines memorize. First step might be set up small *kamidana*—domestic altar—offer prayers, simple reverence gestures. Acquire *ofuda* consecrated shrine, arrange flowers, water, rice, sake. Make silence before space daily, with or without words, but always *magokoro*—true heart. Altar not symbol possession. Reminder presence.

Besides altar, person incorporate routine purification practices. Wash hands, mouth before prayer. Clean house spiritual intention. Practice *misogi* adapted way—conscious morning bath, example. Give thanks before meals. Pay attention nature. Visit trees, rivers, mountains, respect. Listen wind. Stop before sunrise. Small gestures, profoundly transformative. Because Shinto manifests everyday. Not discourses, but silent choices.

Time, visit shrines, participate *matsuri*, learn formal prayers—*norito*—know different kami types, establish affinity some. Study myths, dive symbolic teachings *Kojiki*, *Nihon Shoki*, understand earth origin, creator gods role, light, shadow cycles, order, chaos. Each myth mirror. Each rite mirror. Who looks truth these mirrors begins perceive sacred already self. Shinto recognizes not need reborn live kami. Just open eyes. Just clean mind. Just align gesture intention.

Therefore, no need initiation ceremonies. No authority granting title. Highest authority kami self—reveals inner silence. Heart pure, welcomes. Soul present, remains. No mandatory intermediaries practitioner, divine.

Yes, priests, priestesses. Official rites. Traditional structures. But access kami not conditioned this. Hierarchy exists, not control—serve. Priest guardian rite. *Miko* channel ritual gesture. But common practitioner, even without training, Japanese descent, can live Shinto fully. As long sincerity. Respect. Care beauty, order, silence, space.

Precisely this non-institutionalized character makes conversion intimate experience, often invisible others eyes. Nobody knows, except who lives. Neighbor perceives not. Family notices not. But something changes. Way walking. Way sitting. Way washing dishes. Attention details. Care objects. Gratitude springing even difficult days. Lightness settling gaze. All signs kami presence already found abode.

Countries Shinto little known, silent conversion seem solitary. But never is. Because kami accompany. Need not crowds manifest. Recognize small gesture made whole heart. Where gesture, there space illuminates. There person transforms. There world aligns.

Possible, wishing deepen, contact shrines outside Japan, participate meetings, courses, public ceremonies. Many temples offer instruction, translated materials, respectful welcome. But none mandatory. Just tool. Essential lies daily practice. Cultivating presence. Reverent gaze nature. Respect ancestors. Search purity.

Not rare practitioners other traditions find Shinto bridge, not rupture. Christian continue pray God, learn thank earth Shinto reverence. Buddhist continue meditate, find Shinto rites complementary harmony expression. Skeptic discover, Shinto silent gestures, spirituality demanding not belief—just attention. All, even without renouncing who are, can walk kami.

This coexistence paths, far weakening Shinto, reveals most delicate strength: presence fitting in, welcoming without demanding, transforming without violence. Silent conversion, actually, deep listening. Listening own soul, nature, what vibrates between words. This listening kami approach. No marked day say "now belong," because belonging felt, not proclaimed. Change not name adopted, but way walks world, touches life lighter hands, more attentive eyes.

This lightness, cultivated constancy, overflows all existence spheres. Relations become more respectful, time more sacred, routine less automatic. Spirituality, requiring no oaths nor explicit adhesions, shapes character subtlety, depth. Practitioner not "turns Shinto"—becomes ever more present, attuned impermanence, sensitive what pulses beyond surface. This discreet transformation, world around also changes: because where someone harmony, field harmony being sown.

End, silent conversion flower blooming fanfareless. Perfume shouts not—just transforms air. Who approaches, feels. Perhaps knows not name, recognizes not whence calm comes, gaze brightness, careful gesture. But feels. This feeling, kami make selves perceived. Ask not applause. Ask presence.

Where pure heart acts reverently, there Shinto already flourished—needing not say arrived.

# Chapter 25
# Ancestral Wisdom

Words gods pronounced, gestures made, choices marked early times—all remain alive. Shinto, myths not just past narratives. Spiritual maps, symbolic reflections invisible reality, teachings traversing centuries seeds cast fertile soil human existence. Not stories believe or doubt, but live. Because each myth mirror, who contemplates sees revealed not world distant gods, but own soul motion.

*Kojiki*, *Nihon Shoki*, fundamental texts Shinto thought, contain sacred stories. Narrate Japan birth, gods, natural phenomena, as if all interconnected—and is. When Izanagi, Izanami spun spear primordial ocean, created first land, not just shaping islands. Revealing world born sacred gesture, creation results harmony masculine, feminine, action, receptivity, intention, form. Japan, thus, not profane territory—soil consecrated kami presence origin.

Birth myth Amaterasu, sun goddess, illuminates much more sky. When Izanagi, after descending dead world, purifying self, washes left eye, light born, understands light comes not without pain, inner clarity comes after dive darkness. Amaterasu sun warming, guiding, feeding, but also symbol awakened consciousness, spirit nobility, wisdom revealed looking truth within. Reverence her, still central Shinto, reverence illuminated life, clear path, solar center existing each being.

But no light without shadow, why myth Susanoo, Amaterasu brother, so necessary. Represents storm, chaos, emotional disorder. Impulsive behavior, destructive, instinctive, causes pain, rupture. But also protects, faces dragons, seeks redemption. Untamed aspect soul, needs integrated. When Amaterasu hides cave fear brother, world plunges darkness. But exit ritual—dance, laughter, mirror. Light returns not force—returns beauty, enchantment, reflection. Reflection one greatest Shinto symbols: sacred mirror representing Amaterasu many shrines also symbol awakened self, clear soul, true heart reflecting heaven.

Narrative teaches harmony not absence conflict, but overcoming it. Gods err, fight, distance—but return. Returning, restore world. Movement rupture, recomposition profoundly human. Archetypal. Universal. Why Shinto myths touch contemporary reader such force. Not exotic. Intimate. Portraits soul journey self-knowledge, balance, integration.

Relation gods, humans myths also reveals continuity spheres. No rigid separation. Human ancestors descend kami. Emperors spiritual heirs Amaterasu. Each human carries self divine spark. Therefore, living righteousness, purity, sincerity, also honors spiritual lineage part of. Respect ancestors not just homage—recognition life sustained previous lives. Gestures today echo future generations.

Other myths reveal importance courage, compassion, inner truth. Story Ōkuninushi, example, teaches humility, sacrifice, wisdom. Deceived, suffers, dies, resurrects, end becomes lord invisible world. Trajectory marked trials, losses, but also revelations. Helps injured rabbits, hears spiritual world voices, understands true power born not imposition, but listening. Myth, like many others, power reconfigured: strong be true. Leader be servant common good.

Story goddess Uzume, dancing before Amaterasu cave, making laugh, reminder joy also sacred. Laughter not superficial. Heals. Illuminates. Opens doors. Ritual dance performs, *kagura*, became one most important shrine practices. Because body dancing beauty becomes channel kami. Myth already said.

Ancestral tales not stories others. Revelations how live better, deal shadow, restore light. Myths limit not childhood or Japanese people cultural formation. Remain alive because remain true. Person reading spirit eyes perceives talking them. Fear paralyzing. Anger destroying. Gesture healing. Silence welcoming. Presence transforming. Recognizing self narratives, rediscovers meaning. Rediscovers direction.

Shinto, preserving myths, transforms not dogmas. Offers landscapes. Each traverse own way. See what needs see. Harvest what ready harvest. Returning, brings not answers, but better questions. Because myths explain not—awaken.

Reading *Kojiki*, visiting shrine, reciting *norito*, participating festival, making offering, all part same listening. Myth speaks, but speaks silence. Demands not blind faith. Asks sensitivity. Who develops sensitivity begins perceive life also made symbols. World mirror. Gods continue whispering amidst trees, clouds, dreams, everyday gestures.

Shinto ancestral wisdom light, profound. Weighs not shoulders. Elevates. Corrects not harshly. Guides beauty. Strength lies precisely absence rigidity. Wisdom bending bamboo, breaks not. Renewing seasons. Remaining alive because lives inside each being recognizing it.

The continuity of this wisdom depends not only on preserving ancient texts, but how myths root themselves everyday. When someone chooses silence facing conflict, honors Amaterasu; when welcomes inner chaos patience, dialoguing Susanoo. When dances lightness amidst pain, reverberates Uzume curative audacity. These mythological echoes restrict not ancient Japan—repeat discreetly classrooms, kitchens, forests, markets, temples, everywhere someone remembers live consciously, reverently, courageously.

Most notable this heritage requires not understood rational level. Penetrates sensitive, symbolic, experience. Child observing rice steam rising before altar needs not understand myths intuit something sacred there. Adult walking grove, feeling silent shiver, perhaps never read *Kojiki*, but already, certain way, communion kami. Ancestral wisdom imposes not. Waits. Heart ready, reveals—not theory, but recognition. Remembrance. Reunion.

Following this trail accept invitation live poetically. Listen ancient teachings whispers own heart.

Perceive each simple gesture carry sacred gentle weight. This course, no masters obey, just mirrors contemplate. Clearer reflected image becomes, more practitioner understands: myths tell not distant gods stories. Show paths each human, own steps, find light even shadow—transform life living expression wisdom never dies.

# Chapter 26
# Inner Path

Shinto, so deeply rooted reverence nature, community practices, also contains self core silence. Core showing not easily, but pulses living center whole tradition. Path within path—inner path. Way listening done wordlessly, seeing done effortlessly, feeling done without possessing. Alongside rites, festivals, alongside shrines, priests, exists invisible space encounter divine occurs directly, without intermediaries. Space being interior.

Unlike traditions developing formal meditation techniques, Shinto offers spontaneous, sensory, natural approach contemplation. Imposes not postures, dictates not methods. Invites being. Simply being. Being before river, under tree, before morning mist, there, not world tourist, but part it, allow silence reveal what words reach not. Practice, unsystematized, unnamed, one most profound expressions Shinto spirit. Because it, human withdraws self, same time, finds self.

*Magokoro*—true heart—key this path. Heart seeking not impress, desiring not prove, restless not doubts. Heart simply vibrating harmony what is. Closes not analysis. Opens experience. When state reached, even brief instants, practitioner perceives separation self, world illusory. Tree not there chance. Stone something say. Wind carries ancestral memories. Sky, so vast, fits entirely inside presence instant.

Introspection Shinto not withdrawal escape. Listening way being. Listening occur anywhere: sacred grove quietude, water sound hitting rocks, cicadas song dusk, contemplation garden ordered simplicity. Not about isolating self world. About attuning self world purest state. Why often practitioner prefers not say meditating. Just living attention. Just walking eyes open invisible.

Shinto introspective spirituality finds expression practices like silent shrine visit. No need ask. No need speak. Simple gesture walking towards *torii*, passing through consciously, purifying hands, mouth fresh water, bowing before altar, clapping twice, silencing—all already meditation. Already prayer. Already communion. Body becomes rite. Silence becomes word. Space illuminates, not candles or incense, but real presence what sacred.

Some practitioners develop personal contemplation routines. Wake early greet sun. Not formulas. Presence. Look sky, feel breeze, place feet still damp ground. Make silence minute, three, seven. Short, eternal time, attune what gods saying that day. Others prefer dusk. Sit tree shade, observe light changes, follow breath. No mantra. No desire. Just listening.

Caring space also inner practice. Sweep floor cleans own spirit. Arrange table prepares altar. Wash dishes performs purification ritual. External order echoes internal order. Aesthetics transform ethics.

Beautiful, lived simplicity, reveals sacred path. Home becomes temple. Routine becomes rite. Devotee perceives needs not go far find gods. Because already there, inhabiting each gesture made intention.

This introspective life mode reflected shrine architecture, garden layouts, traditional villages organization. Nothing shouts. Nothing exhibits. Everything welcomes. Everything whispers. Space invites pause. Breath. Presence. Even who knows not rites, understands not symbols, feels touched atmosphere. Because sacred, when real, requires not translation. Touches attentive heart. Attention door inner path.

Japan mountains, retreat places monks, Shinto practitioners seek deeper contact nature, own spirit. Walk silence. Sleep under stars. Drink spring water divine wine. Eat reverence. Not obligation. Because life perceived gift. Living thus, food not just nourishment—gift. Night not just light absence—immersion. Cold not just climate—lesson.

Shinto, even without formalizing meditative methods like Buddhism zazen, teaches form attention transforms. Attention begins body. Breath. Way walking. Way sitting. Care what touched. Body, slowed down, lived consciously, becomes revelation instrument. Devotee learns, gradually, what sought always closer imagined.

Inner path, therefore, most accessible, most demanding. Needs not grand rites, but requires real presence. Requires not deep knowledge, but requires truth. Imposes not dogmas, but invites constant listening. Who accepts invitation, even once day, even few minutes, discovers kami speak silence. Universe its language. Soul, when hears, finds peace.

This contemplative dimension essential modern life balance. Amidst noise, rush, excess stimuli, Shinto proposes pause. Not escape world, but rediscover self in it. Practitioner living attentive nature cycles, gratitude small things, respect inner rhythms, transforms presence. Presence, itself, already offering. Already prayer. Already bridge between worlds.

In the silent paths of Shinto, everyday life reveals itself as a succession of sacred portals. Each gesture, each attentive gaze, each instant of full presence, becomes an opportunity for reverence. No need seek outside what pulses within: kami, inhabiting trees, stones, springs, also inhabit breath now. Thus, cultivating interiority not distancing life, but deepening it—feeling simple sacred, ordinary contains extraordinary, true listening transforms even most banal moments living communion.

This awareness extends beyond individual, radiating bonds others, world. Care environment, gentleness gestures, respect things' timing: all become expression inner path. What previously seemed trivial—sweeping floor, preparing tea, lighting lantern—acquires spiritual density. Silence ceases absence sound become dense, living, receptive presence. Like tranquil water surface, mirrors not just sky, but also deepest feelings, only revealing when no rush.

This state simple, sincere attention, devotee perceives inner path leads not another place, but deepens place where is. Spiritual journey not ladder upwards, but dive present. There, center now, between clapping hands, wind sound, fresh water touch, morning sky gaze, soul recognizes already home. No separation sacred, everyday. Only presence.

# Chapter 27
# Beauty as Path

Essential delicacy permeates every aspect Shinto. Not ostentation, not artifice. Contained beauty, almost invisible, absolutely present. Light gesture arranging flower altar. Way *torii* rises against sky. Roof curve following clouds contour. Stone arrangement garden where each element seems found place itself. This beauty, so discreet, powerful, not just aesthetic reflection—spiritual trail. Shinto, beauty path. Path sacred, path heart, path kami presence.

Perception beauty spiritual experience deeply rooted Japanese sensitivity, especially idea *wabi-sabi*. *Wabi* modest simplicity, elegance essential, contentment what is. *Sabi* beauty time passage, imperfection acceptance, transience value. Together, form aesthetic celebrating what unfinished, aged, transforms. Cracked cup, worn wood, fallen leaf stone—all, observed reverence, become divine mirror.

Shinto separates not beautiful sacred. What beautiful, lived purity, automatically expression divine presence. Why sacred spaces impose not. Integrate. Shrine built not dominate landscape, but converse it. Path leading surrounded trees, wind sound part liturgy, light filtered leaves becomes natural illumination.

Nature not frame—temple body. Beauty revealing there not fabricated. Revealed.

Living Shinto learn perceive beauty. Become sensitive invisible. Slow gaze, clean mind, allow world present self interference. Learning requires not technical knowledge. Requires attention. Flower blooming path work. Subtle utensil arrangement table. Way shadow projects tatami dusk. Nothing banal. Everything manifestation. Who sees eyes offering transforms each instant cult.

Everyday, thus, becomes territory aesthetic, spiritual expression. Arrange house carefully. Clean forgotten corner zealously. Choose object intention. Keep space ordered. Prepare meal attention details. Dress sobriety, beauty. All, done *magokoro*, cult. Way attune kami flow. Because gods demand not marble temples. Feel comfortable where harmony.

Harmony not uniform. Excludes not irregular. Conversely, *wabi-sabi* teaches precisely asymmetry, impermanence, rusticity, beauty flourishes more truth. Falling leaf marks time. Moss covering stone reveals days silence. Old house creaking wind speaks lives passed there. Shinto honors time. Honors memory. Honors what ages dignity. Because what carries history carries spirit. Where spirit, kami.

Rituals, even simplest, permeated aesthetic reverence. Altar not pile symbols—clean space, airy, balanced. Vase water, *sakaki* branch, bowl rice, candle, perhaps incense. Nothing excess. Nothing lacking. Space between objects important objects themselves.

Attention form educates spirit. Teaches excess disturbs. Noise distances. Beauty needs silence reveal self.

Larger ceremonies, aesthetic amplifies. Priests clothes, choreographed gestures, musical instruments, *miko* movements—all dance. All care. No rush. No distraction. Time extends. Mind quiets. Body becomes sacred vehicle. Beauty, here, not spectacle. Connection means. Serves not enchant eyes. Serves open heart.

Even writing *norito*, formal prayers, follows principle. Poetic words, rhythmic, almost musical. Spoken calm voice, continuous, enveloping. Sound has weight. Silence between sounds depth. Meaning not just content—form. Form, lived sincerity, creates presence field. Kami hears. Practitioner feels. Harmony established.

Home, sensitivity manifests small gestures. Way flower placed *genkan*, house entrance. Way kitchen organized. Object arrangement *kamidana*. Care cleaning. Utensil choice. Nothing neutral. Everything communicates. Everything vibrates. Environment vibrates harmony, soul quiets. House becomes temple. Day becomes rite.

Valorization discreet beauty also teaches deal aging, imperfection, finitude. Chipped cup not thrown away. Repaired gold—technique known *kintsugi*. Golden scar becomes piece most beautiful part. Because pain hidden not. Transformed art. Life, losses, marks, equally worthy. Aging face. Changing body. Breaking heart. All redone. All shine.

Shinto aesthetic, therefore, not luxury. Ethics. Interiorization path. Gaze discipline. Soul purification gesture. Who cultivates gaze begins see world other eyes. Begins hear leaves sound. Perceive dust dance light. Feel tea warmth blessing. Begins be, truly be, where is.

Shinto invites this presence. Live not just function, but beauty. Work not just obligation, but harmony. Inhabit spaces not just necessity, but reverence. When becomes natural, simplest gesture carries spirit, person becomes sacred channel. Walking rite. Silence prayer. House altar. Life, path.

Beauty, when welcomed as a way of spiritual expression, reveals itself not as adornment, but as a mode of listening. Listening to the world, listening to oneself, listening to the kami. In this state of awakened sensitivity, the contrasts between simplicity and depth disappear: a gnarled trunk becomes a teaching; a shadow lengthening at day's end, a reminder that everything passes. The gaze refined by Shinto aesthetics is, simultaneously, a gaze that heals—because it seeks not to correct the imperfect, but sees in it a form of truth. Beauty, then, ceases to be something contemplated from outside and becomes something inhabited from within.

This way of inhabiting the world silently transforms the everyday. And transforms the subject too. What was previously executed hastily becomes sacred practice. What was previously discarded is now repaired with affection. Beauty ceases to be a function of youth or symmetry and converts into a matter of presence and intention. The soul attuned to this vibration finds serenity even amidst impermanence. After all, when one understands everything is flow—light, body, emotion—it is finally possible to rest in the moment with gratitude. Time, then, ceases to be enemy and becomes frame for revelations.

Thus, living by beauty is not futility—it is courage. Courage to open eyes to the ephemeral and find something eternal in it. Courage to recognize the divine in humblest details. Courage to surrender to gesture truthfully. When walking becomes dance, silence becomes music, gaze becomes blessing, one perceives beauty is not in things, but way seeing them. And this way, so intimate, silent, soul touches most sacred.

## Chapter 28
## Spirit of Gratitude

Heart Shinto, pulses soft, invisible, powerful force. Force depending not elaborate rituals, nor complex words. Force reach any person, place, moment. Force gratitude. Not occasional feeling, but continuous state consciousness. Not response favor received, but silent recognition existence gift. Gratitude, Shinto, not just virtue—living bridge human, divine.

First day moments, practitioner invited thank. Opening eyes, feeling sunlight, hearing wind or rain sound, breathing deeply, opportunity reverence. Body awakening, house sheltering, food waiting, work calling, all gifts. Each gift, recognized such, strengthens link kami. Because gods demand not grandiose offerings. Make selves present when sincere gratitude exists.

Gratitude expresses simple gestures. Head bow before *kamidana*. Conscious breath before meal. Attentive gaze sky late afternoon. Light touch tree passing. Deep sigh before flower bloomed. Brief moments, full presence. Presence transforms everything. Because when truly present, perceives nothing guaranteed. Everything gift. Recognition opens heart.

Prayers Shinto, mostly, prayers thanksgiving. Devotee approaches not shrine just ask. Goes, above all, thank. Thank what received, what not happen, what learned, what possible. Thank even what not understood. Because life flow, even what seems loss contain blessing. Kami know paths human sees not. Trusting them also act gratitude.

Festivals, grateful dimension takes body. *Niiname-sai*, example, one oldest, most sacred rites, emperor offers gods first rice harvest, name entire people. Before eating, offers. Before enjoying, reveres. Natural order things Shinto: first, recognize. Then, receive. One thanking becomes worthy what possesses. One just demanding, breaks flow.

Ethics gratitude shapes Japanese culture profoundly. Habit thanking before, after meals—*itadakimasu, gochisōsama*—not mere formality. Living expression respect food, preparer work, lives beings transformed sustenance. Thank fish, rice, farmer, cook, fire, earth, time. Meal not banal. Ritual. Food, received consciously, nourishes more than body—nourishes spirit.

Same way, work initiated thanksgiving. Week begins formal greetings, reverence gestures, rituals companies, stores. Many establishments maintain active *kamidana*, offerings water, salt, rice. Each morning, restart gratitude. Something works right, celebrates. Something fails, learns. Both cases, thanks. Because living already reason this.

Shrines themselves spaces collective gratitude. *Ema*, small wooden plaques faithful write wishes or thanks, accumulate altars thousands silent messages. "Thank you health," "healing," "my child's life," "this year ending," "love rediscovered." Each plaque testimony spirituality needs not extraordinary miracles. Needs eyes seeing gift what common.

Gratitude also manifests care ancestors. Visiting tombs, cleaning memorials, offering flowers, incense, devotee not just fulfilling duty. Expressing gratitude own existence. Each life continuity. Each birth bridge. Who recognizes lineage preceding lives more respect, humility, balance.

Grateful spirit denies not suffering. Shinto romanticizes not pain. Teaches, even pain, space gratitude. Gratitude strength arising. Gratitude hands helping. Gratitude time healing. Gratitude consciousness maturing. When gratitude settles, pain becomes not smaller—heart becomes larger.

Daily practice gratitude profound effects. Organizes mind, purifies gaze, aligns being. Person thanking lives less weight. Complains less. Demands less. Compares self less. Feels part flow. Feels accompanied. Feels full. Because gratitude kami language. Speak not loud voice. Respond sincerity. Who thanks, listens. Who thanks, receives more. Not because asked—because became capable recognize.

Practice requires not great transformations. Begins waking, looking sky. Opening window, letting air enter. Saying "thank you" intention. Writing three reasons thank end day. Remembering who present. Touching beloved object respect. Everything field gratitude. Each instant thus lived becomes altar.

Kami ask not perfection. Ask presence. Gratitude purest form presence. Not spectacle. State. Silent vibration transforming environment. Making ground firmer. Clearing thought. Healing resentment. Dissolving selfishness. Gratitude opposite forgetting. Recognition. Who recognizes lives other way. Walks other lightness. Breathes other depth.

Shinto, living gratitude living communion world. Perceiving life, even imperfections, generous. Time teacher. Death part cycle. Others presence blessing. Simple sufficient. Now, lived attention, gratitude, already contains everything.

Gratitude, when fully lived, transforms existence into constant reciprocity. No separation between giver and receiver, offered and what offered return. Everything mixes same gesture: rice nourishing, earth sustaining, sun warming—human heart which, recognizing, returns world not just words, but presence. Silent dance giving, thanking, daily living becomes celebration, not great events, but miracle hidden details, sacred hiding simple. Gratitude, thus understood, much more than response: way being world.

This way shapes gaze. Who lives gratitude learns see more clearly, feel more wholly, hear more listening. Complaints lose space, not repression, but because soul changes frequency. World, all contrasts, perceived place learning, revelation. Even difficult encounters leave wisdom traces. Even losses, light remains lit—not denial, but understanding. When spirit turns recognition what is, instead expectation what lacks, sprouts peace depending not guarantees. Peace born bond own impermanence.

This state, life ceases path demands become path welcoming. Walking becomes lighter. Not because weights disappear, but heart aligns what essential: existence gift, others presence, nature generosity, kami silence. Gratitude, finally, not end—fertile soil spirituality flourishes. Where human meets divine noiselessly. Where instant reveals whole. Where simple suffices.

# Chapter 29
# The Way of Harmony

Heart Shinto vibrates word needing not said loud voice understood. Word present silent forests, carefully arranged gardens, rituals performed synchrony, respectful gesture two people meeting. Word *wa*—harmony. More than concept, *wa* state. Common breath beings, things. Rhythm organizing chaos without nullifying diversity. Invisible line sewing sky earth, individual community, gesture silence. Through harmony world maintained. Through it kami make selves present.

Living harmony living balance everything exists. Not just people, but spaces, time, ancestors, natural rhythms. Shinto separates not existence domains. What outside reverberates inside. What done body affects environment. What thought resonates bonds. Therefore, each action, however small seems, spiritual weight. Way room arranged, path walked, meal served, story listened—all either strengthens or breaks harmony.

Awareness begins early. Childhood, Japanese educated perceive presence impact collective. Learns not be burden others. Space order reflection inner order. Talking excess injure others silence. Acting inattentively disturbs flow. Not repression—attunement. Soul tuned instrument. Harmony, when touched, transforms environment temple.

Shinto shrines, harmony lived extreme care element arrangement. Nothing there chance. *Torii* not just portal—alignment. Stone path not just trail—preparation entry sacred space. Purification font not there ornament—rite rediscover center. Passing spaces attention, devotee feels rebalanced. Inner world organized outer world order. Body, slowing, returns listen life flow.

Harmony also reveals human relations. Shinto deeply values mutual respect, discreet kindness, silent cooperation. Conflict denied not, treated delicately. Anger recognized, not amplified. Disagreement welcomed, not celebrated. Because everything unbalancing distances kami. Gods descend not where excessive noise. Prefer places gesture clear, word measured, heart true.

Emphasis harmony makes Shinto relational spirituality. Person saves not self alone. Saves self restoring bonds. Nature. Others. Own essence. Guilt, here, not punitive feeling—sign something misaligned. Shame, context, self-perception tool. Perceiving attitude hurt things order, seeks correct. Seeks ask forgiveness. Seeks purify. Because purity not just physical—harmony restored.

Harmony nature another fundamental axis. Forests preserved not just ecological reasons, but kami abode. Mountains respected living entities. Rivers revered. Stones left place. Shinto teaches meddling world without listening generates disorder. Building excess, extracting carelessly, consuming unconsciously, breaks sacred pact earth. Where pact broken, void settles. Abundance vanishes. Soul sickens.

Therefore, even large cities, shrines. Small harmony refuges. Spaces bell sound cuts car noise. Where wind blows unhurriedly. Where kami presence restorative. Places not just memory. Spiritual lungs. Spaces time aligns again. Where rush dissolves. Where human remembers part something larger.

Shinto teaches also restoring harmony always possible. No matter how much erred. Important recognize. Purify. Return. Impurity not malice—discordance. Rite exists help human rediscover rhythm. *Misogi*, water cleaning, more than bath—gesture return fluidity state. Water takes what weighs. What weighs too much, distances gods lightness.

Vision influences even aesthetics. Beauty not symmetry. Dynamic balance. Order welcoming unforeseen. Floral arrangement, example, made considering void between elements. Garden seeks not control nature—enhance it. Well-kept environment not one everything shines, but where everything breathes together. Breathing, when shared, becomes spiritual experience.

Harmony also cultivated social structures. Community organization, elder respect, shared responsibility public tasks, all reflect coexistence spirituality. Festivals, harmony manifests neighbor cooperation, collective dance, food division, common life celebration. Kami invoked, not one property, but presence all. Neighborhood well-being seen everyone well-being.

Times crisis, harmony culture shows strength. Natural tragedies, scarcity moments, people unite. Organize. Cooperate. Silence. Wait. Help. Not because demanded—because learned early balance built together. Suffering, shared, weighs less. Pain, recognized, generate compassion.

Restoring harmony, when broken, requires courage. Humility. Listening. Silence. Shinto abandons not who errs. Offers paths. Reconciliation paths. Purification paths. Return paths. Who returns, sincerity, finds gods again. Because kami patient. Wait. Observe. Welcome.

Living Way Harmony living expanded consciousness. Perceiving each action vibrates. Each word builds or destroys. Each choice echoes. Therefore, Shinto practitioner seeks, everything, balance. Not perfection. Continuous adjustment. Like boat correcting course each wave. Like tree bending wind, breaks not.

True harmony strength resides persistent softness. Imposes not, but invites. Forces not, but sustains. Therefore, often passes unnoticed—foundation holding house upright, breath giving body life. Practitioner living attentive principle understands harmony not fixed state, but living process listening, response. Each day, situation, requires new attunement gesture: extra silence, fewer words, choice considering not just own good, but good all sharing same space. Harmony, thus, becomes spiritual compass.

This way living, based relational awareness, transforms how reacts world. Instead reacting impulsively, learns respond presence. Instead imposing, seeks understand. Not about nullifying own desires, but placing dialogue whole. Anger finds listening. Frustration finds care. Joy finds sharing. Harmony not emotional anesthesia—alchemy. Transforms without erasing. Educates without repressing. Process, human becomes not just spiritual tradition practitioner, but pacifying presence world.

Living way harmony, therefore, daily choice way existing uniting, welcoming, rebalancing. Cultivation life seeking not control, but connection. Where error not definitive failure, but return opportunity. Where beauty born respect, ethics springs affection. Path, practitioner understands no gesture too small restore world order. Suffices attentive gaze, conscious step, open heart—kami presence flourishes.

# Chapter 30
# Eternity of the Kami

Shinto, time not straight line separating past, present, future. Circle, spiral, cosmic breath. Pulses cycles: seasons, generations, lives. Within cycles, permanence. Silent continuity depending not matter, nor memory. Presence remaining, even human eyes no longer see. Kami, nature gods, forces, ancestors, disappear not. Remain. Not bodies, not fixed forms, but spirit. Essence. Vibration. Because Shinto, sacred eternal.

Eternity not abstract idea. Lived rituals, gestures, landscapes, bonds. Expresses constant ancestor reverence, shrines traversing centuries, sacred trees witnessed entire generations passing under shadow. Time, these spaces, seems suspended. Altar stone same five hundred years. Bell, rung dawn, resonates resonated centuries ago. *Torii*, crossed silence, opens same portal between worlds. Nothing changed. Everything remains. Because everything state continuity.

Idea ancestors become kami after death one most profound expressions eternity. Not belief reincarnation, nor soul theology. Recognition: what lived purity, sincerity, righteousness, remains. One lived *makoto* disappears not. Becomes presence. Silent influence.

Protective spirit. Kami. Transformation not privilege few. Reach all. Shinto teaches anyone, living virtue, remembered reverence. Become inspiration source, protection, guidance. Grandfather cared family. Mother prayed before *kamidana*. Village elder preserved rituals. Farmer respected earth. All, departing, go not. Remain. Not shadow, but light.

Light lit each domestic altar, each rice offering, each flower left before grave. Memory not burden—bridge. Ancestor spirit demands not adoration, just recognition. Respect given past seed future. Thus, time curves self. Present enriched presence who came before.

Ancestor worship rituals, eternity made tangible. Naming dead loud voice, reciting gratitude words, offering water, incense, food, practitioner places self before time mystery. Simple gesture, understands not alone. Life continuation. Blood carries stories. Gestures reverberate future generations. Becomes link. Link, when conscious, sacred.

Vision also offers different way understand death. Shinto, not definitive rupture. Transition. Loss pain exists, paralyzes not. Grief lived reverence, silence, cleanliness. Body cared, spirit guided. Remembrance cultivated. Altar deceased name remains. Tomb visits become encounters. Spirit called not—already there. What offered gratitude.

Kami eternity also manifests nature. Mountains, rivers, winds, stars—all expressions continuous sacred. Stone ages not. Sea ceases not. Sky disappears not. Change, but remain. Human, recognizing, aligns greater time. Ceases live just immediate. Passes respect cycles, honor what came before, care what come after. Care way eternalize own existence. Not monuments, not fame, but actions.

Shinto teaches living well living way presence makes difference. Gesture inspires. Name awakens respect. Passage earth leaves harmony trail. When happens, death not end—return. Return great cycle. Return kami flow. Return invisible field whence everything came, where everything goes.

Therefore, gods age not. Die not. Transform, move, withdraw. But remain. Each blooming flower, each warming sunbeam, each breeze touching face tenderness. World full kami because world full life. Where life lived reverence, eternity.

Perception transforms how lives. Act not just self. Acts consciousness each attitude resonates. Good practiced perpetuates. Care generates roots. Gratitude opens paths. Thus, even simplest gestures—sweeping temple, caring garden, helping neighbor—become eternity seeds. Human time brief. What done truth remains.

Shinto promises not eternal life another world. Invites build eternity here. What touched, offered, left. Immortality, this path, not death escape. Presence continuity. Who lives consciousness continuity, lives more lightness, depth, peace.

Kami eternity also call. Call live way life continues beyond body. Way name remembered affection. Way presence missed. Way spirit becomes light. Not vanity. Devotion. Humility. Sincere desire leave world better found.

This eternity consciousness, so present Shinto, dissolves death fear without denying pain. Life end not disappearance—transformation. Accepting transformation reverence, human learns welcome also everyday small deaths: cycle end, bond loss, inner landscape change. Everything going, remains somehow. Everything silencing, echoes other planes. Thus, life ceases line running final point, passes circle expanding. Flow renewing.

Living this perception changes way being world. Choices become more conscious, bonds deeper, gestures more significant. Because each word echo beyond instant, each action inscribe time. Kami eternity not static—living continuity. What maintained through care, memory, intention. Understanding each instant permanence seed, no more space existence waste. Present becomes sacred ground. Now becomes altar.

This sense, eternity not beyond—between. Between generations, worlds, one gesture, another. Practitioner living consciousness subtle presence understands spirit ends not death, transforms silent influence, guiding wind, consoling remembrance. Thus, cycle closes, restarts, peace. Because life, lived *makoto*, needs not last forever—suffices been whole.

# Chapter 31
# Wisdom of the Cycles

In Shinto, nothing is fixed. Nothing is static. Nothing remains as it was. What blooms will one day fall. What begins will one day end. But the end is never absolute termination—it is transition. It is an inflection point in the great movement guiding all things. The universe moves not in a straight line. It breathes. It spins. It returns. And in this incessant return, humans find not the monotony of repetition, but the profound wisdom of renewal. This is the wisdom of cycles. Wisdom learned not from books, but absorbed through coexistence with nature, with time, with life itself.

The seasons are an expression of this wisdom. Spring arrives with its promise of rebirth. Summer expands everything. Autumn gathers. Winter silences. And each phase, however ephemeral, is full in its truth. The modern error is wanting to fixate on a single season. Wanting only warmth, only light, only blossoming. But Shinto teaches there is beauty in every phase. That the fallen leaf has as much value as the budding sprout. That snow covering the earth is not absence of life—it is fertile rest. That cold prepares the blossoming.

This teaching extends to human life. There are times of expansion and times of withdrawal. Times of creation and times of waiting. Times of intense joy and times of deep pain. All are part of the same flow. Attempting to resist the cycle is what generates suffering. Wisdom lies in trusting. Trusting pain will pass. Light will return. Heart will find new rhythm. This trust is not passivity. It is alignment. Active acceptance. Listening to the greater rhythm guiding everything.

Childhood, youth, maturity, old age are seasons of the soul. Each carries its brilliance. Each its weight. Shinto invites honoring them all. Childhood with purity, freshness. Youth with boldness. Maturity with silent strength. Old age with accumulated wisdom. None superior. None inferior. All expressions of kami in motion. Who lives each reverently, lives fully.

This cyclical awareness also changes how one views failure, loss, error. None definitive. All can be redone. Restarted. Purified. Shinto, idea *harae*, purification, allows human free self past weight. Not about erasing—about cleaning. Letting go. Letting be. Error recognized, purified becomes seed correctness. Pain welcomed becomes source compassion. Loss lived truth opens space new.

Rituals, festivals, wisdom manifests beauty. *Shōgatsu*, Japanese New Year, not just party—renewal rite. Houses cleaned. Previous year amulets burned. New year first sunrays greeted silence, reverence. Everything begins again. Restart lived not obligation, but blessing. Because living chance try again. Be little better. Walk more truth.

Shinto teaches pain also part path. Suffering not punishment. Passage. Part purification preceding blossoming. Cherry blossom, supreme symbol Japanese beauty, so admired precisely because lasts short time. Beauty lies ephemerality. So with everything life. Love. Youth. Presence loved one. All temporary. But nothing vain. What lived intensity remains, even after gone.

Wisdom cycles also expressed relation nature. Farmer planting knows wait. Forces not time. Respects earth. Knows seed has rhythm. Sprout needs sun, shade. Harvest only comes who cares patience. Shinto practitioner learns field. Learns trust. Learns work without attachment. Learns harvest gratitude. Because everything coming, comes kami. Everything going, also returns him.

Vision generates ethics presence. Person ceases live search ideal future. Passes inhabit now reverence. Present, however common seems, only time sacred reveals. Walk temple, rain sound roof, tea drunk silence, gesture sweeping floor—all rite. All cycle. All opportunity live attention.

Shinto offers not promises immutable eternity. Offers eternity cycles. Certainty everything returns. Light returns. Life renews. Certainty requires not blind faith. Requires open eyes. Present heart. Awakened body. Attributes anyone cultivate, anywhere, anytime.

Difficult phases, wisdom shield. Everything seems stagnant, practitioner remembers: nothing remains. What weighs today, tomorrow dissolves. What darkens today, tomorrow brightens. Wheel turns. Tide changes. Wind blows. Kami, silent, accompanies. Imposes not. Hurries not. But sustains. Sustenance, even invisible, real force.

Living cycles wisdom living humility. Recognizing controls not everything. Possesses nothing. Everything coming present. Everything going, takes part what learned. Loss not void—space new. End not defeat—invitation transformation. Falling leaves not death—preparation another flowering.

Thus, Shinto leads practitioner more serene life. Not absence challenges, but confidence flow. Presence instants. Gratitude even silence. Joy not noisy, but constant. Because who lives consciousness cycles, learns dance life. Walk gods. Repose existence rhythm.

Recognition cycles divine expression also teaches live more compassion—not just self, but others. Understanding each person traverses own seasons, becomes easier welcome fragilities, winters, pauses. Rush yields listening. Demand transforms care. Judgment gives way understanding. Other error no longer seen unforgivable failure, but part path formation, seed yet flower its time. Nobody always summer, nobody free autumn winds. Shared consciousness generates bonds tenderer, more human, truer.

Living subtle perception, everything gains new value. Instants cease mere steps something greater pass place revelation itself. Everyday becomes sacred expression. Cooking, walking, caring house, listening someone, crying, laughing, resting—all intertwine invisible thread connecting human sacred. Shinto practitioner learns honor threads. Seeks not escape world, but dive presence.

Living cycles, sense, accept self part universal dance. Not spectator, but participant. Leaf falling, flower born, wind blowing, passing, transforms. Continuous flow finds fuller way existing—not based rigid certainties or fixed goals, but existence molding time, water learning stone contour. Wisdom cycles not formula, experience. Not doctrine, felt experience. Invites, silently, deep listening life. Who hears call learns beauty even loss, meaning even silence, path even when sees no road. Because everything returns. Return, being remakes self.

# Chapter 32
# The Living Legacy

Shinto is not an echo of the past. It is not kept in showcases, nor belongs only ancient books. Sleeps not under history ashes, nor rests forgotten temples. Shinto lives. Breathes. Grows. Reveals self simplest gesture, deepest silence, most everyday life. Needs not conversion, nor dogmas, nor discourses. Suffices attentive gaze, sincere heart, awakened presence. Because kami, silent gods creation, continue among us. Distanced not. Just wait. Wait recognized water gleam, mountain firmness, wind whisper. Wait greeted respect, not complex words, but true attitudes. Demand not perfect rituals—accept imperfect gesture made truth. Shinto this: spirituality imposing not. Invites. Demanding not. Inspires. Speaking not loud. But when listened, transforms.

Legacy not exclusive property Japanese people. Born Japan, yes. Rooted land, culture, way living. But truths universal. Every human live reverence. Every heart cultivate purity. Every soul learn see sacred natural world. Every home become altar. Every day lived rite. When happens, Shinto ceases foreign religion—becomes inner path.

Path requires not practitioner abandon other beliefs. Competes not. Disputes not. Condemns not. Welcomes who walks sincerity. Desires live gratitude. Recognizes world beauty. Acts respect. Listens attention. Shinto no central headquarters. No prophet. No commandment book. Has mountains. Rivers. Seasons cycle. Sunlight, trees shadow. Has human heart, where each gesture sacred.

Shinto legacy legacy harmony. World. Others. Self. Living well living balance. Respecting limits. Caring what has. Thanking what arrives. Accepting what goes. Honoring ancestors. Protecting who come. Time, Shinto, not rush. Continuity. Who understands, lives without fear. Knows what true never lost. Just transforms.

Teaching present way lives everyday. Way enters house. Arranges table. Greets day. Retires night. Nothing banal. Everything occasion presence. World, seen Shinto eyes, temple. Living world, itself, form prayer.

Shrines, even smallest, continue receiving visitors. Priests continue performing rites. *Miko* still dance. People still clap, still bow before *torii*, still leave offerings, still ask protection, still thank. Even those not born Japan, never visited temple, perhaps know not kami names, can participate flow. Because sacred, lived truth, manifests anywhere.

*Kamidana*, domestic altar, raised any home. Suffices clean space. Intention gesture. Plant branch. Water glass. Silence moment. There, between four walls, invisible approaches. Gods presence depends not geography. Depends purity. Depends sincerity. Depends gratitude.

Shinto teaches living well not accumulation. Connection. Having much not peace guarantee. But living respect yes. Natural world not obstacle—mirror. True spirituality proclaims not—lives. Silence. Beauty. Harmony.

Legacy available whoever wants. Needs not title. Needs not initiation. Needs just will live more truth. Listen wind. Respect time. Care life. Keep heart open. Choice made, kami approach. Because recognize *magokoro*—true heart. Impressed not appearance. Rejoice integrity.

Shinto ended not. Weakened not. Disappeared not. Just continues being what always was: silent path sacred. Continuous presence everyday. Reminder living can be lighter, more beautiful, purer. Each step, when taken reverence, also step taken gods.

This is legacy. Way walking. Way living. Sensitivity. Silence healing. Beauty demanding not. Purity transforming. Path never ending. Because Way Kami always restarting. Each gesture. Each season. Each heart choosing live sincerity.

The vitality of Shinto resides not only in preserving its rites or repeating its practices—it pulses in how it transforms the gaze. The attentive practitioner begins see with other eyes, not because learned something new, but because began remember what, some level, always knew. Reverence before rain, silent respect ancient stone, gratitude simple food—all springs not rule, but recognition: world inhabited subtle presences, everything deserves care.

This gaze change requires not dramatic effort. Insinuates self. Happens day folds, body rhythm, time listening. Why Shinto, even discreet, leaves deep marks. Seeks not occupy space, but generate meaning. Pretends not dominate, but awaken. Legacy lives where someone willing live intention. Matters not temple between mountains or urban apartment; among ancestral trees or concrete walls—what matters gesture quality. Consciousness living. Nobility simplicity. Above all, cultivation *magokoro*, true heart exhibiting not, but offering. Where heart flourishes, path present. There kami approach, not distant figures, but inseparable part pulsing life.

Following this path accept sacred not far, nor hidden—here, now, accessible whoever wants see. Reveals silent care small things, respect what not understood, gratitude what simply is. Shinto legacy needs not carried flag. Transmits way being world. Living heritage. Like all living, continues moving, growing, finding new spaces, forms, hearts where flourish.

# Epilogue

Reaching end this journey, something you changed. Perhaps imperceptible eyes, but clear soul. Like cherry blossom falling silence, yet transforming ground rests upon—so too words, rites, gestures, kami presented here landed gently your inner world. Now, everything vibrates differently.

What read not manual, nor treatise. Revelation. Subtle call presence. More that: remembrance. Because, deep down, already knew. Knew exists something sacred way breeze touches face, way water runs between fingers, sound silence between words. Shinto just returned you forgotten knowing, dormant under layers rush, noise, logic.

Learned, pages, sacred separated not everyday. Divine dwells not only temples, but lives simple gestures, pure objects, sincere instants. Learned spirituality needs not promises, but practice; not blind faith, but *magokoro*—true heart.

Reached here, did not just reader. Became pilgrim. Each chapter step towards new way being world. Crossed portals, revered ancestral gods, contemplated festivals celebrations life, impermanence. Felt purity not moralistic concept, but vibrational state. Understood offering not giving, but thanking already received. Perhaps most important: recognized no separation you, world. All that is, is together.

Spirituality pulsing each rite, dance, prayer, sacred sound, now pulses also you. Cannot be undone.

Japan, silent reverence, aesthetic sense impregnated sacredness, not just country—mirror. Reflection what happens entire people decides live attention, gratitude, respect nature, invisible. Living reminder true prosperity measured not just figures or conquests, but harmony what transcends us. Harmony begins, saw, home. Domestic altar water renewed carefully. Cleaning done not just sanitize, but purify. Act eating reverence. Gaze cast sky dawn. Entire world, then, reveals sanctuary. Each life, offering construction.

Internalizing teachings this book, not just absorbing foreign wisdom. Rescuing forgotten sensitivity—ancestral form living communion everything breathes, grows, flows, transforms. Assuming new commitment: listen world more delicately, act more presence, exist more gratitude.

Because now know: Wind blows not vain. Stone not there chance. Silence not empty. And you... ... you bridge between worlds.

Kami everywhere—but shout not. Wait. Wait right gesture, respectful posture, aligned heart. Wait you each morning, each kindness act, each word spoken truth. Knowing this, become active part great sacred field sustaining universe.

Nothing ends here. Contrary: now begins what essential.

Permit self return previous chapters revisits garden: each season, reveals new flowers. Same happen this book. More you transform, more reveal. Because wisdom contained pages not linear—cyclical, alive, organic.

You can close book. Cannot close eyes anymore.

Bell sound still echoes. Breeze still carries messages. Flower still falls silence.

And you, now knowing hear invisible, walk not alone anymore.

www.ingramcontent.com/pod-product-compliance
Lightning Source LLC
LaVergne TN
LVHW041943070526
838199LV00051BA/2890